2nd Workshop on Metaphor in NLP 2014

Held at ACL 2014

Baltimore, Maryland, USA
26 June 2014

ISBN: 978-1-63439-203-7

Printed from e-media with permission by:

Curran Associates, Inc.
57 Morehouse Lane
Red Hook, NY 12571

CURRAN ASSOCIATES INC.
proceedings
.com

Some format issues inherent in the e-media version may also appear in this print version.

Printed by Curran Associates, Inc. (2014)

Association for Computational Linguistics
209 N. Eighth Street
Stroudsburg, Pennsylvania 18360

Phone: 1-570-476-8006
Fax: 1-570-476-0860

acl@aclweb.org

Additional copies of this publication are available from:

Curran Associates, Inc.
57 Morehouse Lane
Red Hook, NY 12571 USA
Phone: 845-758-0400
Fax: 845-758-2634
Email: curran@proceedings.com
Web: www.proceedings.com

Introduction

Characteristic to all areas of human activity (from poetic to ordinary to scientific) and, thus, to all types of discourse, metaphor becomes an important problem for natural language processing. Its ubiquity in language has been established in a number of corpus studies and the role it plays in human reasoning has been confirmed in psychological experiments. This makes metaphor an important research area for computational and cognitive linguistics, and its automatic identification and interpretation indispensable for any semantics-oriented NLP application.

The work on metaphor in NLP and AI started in the 1980s, providing us with a wealth of ideas on the structure and mechanisms of the phenomenon. The last decade witnessed a technological leap in natural language computation, whereby manually crafted rules gradually give way to more robust corpus-based statistical methods. This is also the case for metaphor research. In the recent years, the problem of metaphor modeling has been steadily gaining interest within the NLP community, with a growing number of approaches exploiting statistical techniques. Compared to more traditional approaches based on hand-coded knowledge, these more recent methods tend to have a wider coverage, as well as be more efficient, accurate and robust. However, even the statistical metaphor processing approaches so far often focused on a limited domain or a subset of phenomena. At the same time, recent work on computational lexical semantics and lexical acquisition techniques, as well as a wide range of NLP methods applying machine learning to open-domain semantic tasks, open many new avenues for creation of large-scale robust tools for recognition and interpretation of metaphor.

This year's workshop is the second workshop focused on modeling of metaphor using NLP techniques, following the first workshop held at NAACL 2013. The 2013 workshop turned out to be a popular event, with 28 registered participants and more people in attendance. In 2013, accepted papers dealt with metaphor annotation, features for metaphor identification, and with generalization of the techniques across languages. These themes continue to be represented in this year's workshop, along with additional foci on interpretation, applications, and relationships with related phenomena. We received 11 submissions and accepted 7, based on detailed and careful reviews by members of the Program Committee.

Two of the accepted papers deal with aspects of interpretation, such as the affect carried by the metaphor (Strzalkowski et al) and the underlying plausible reasoning mechanisms such as abduction (Ovchinnikova et al). Another theme is the application of metaphor to support creative exploration of language and ideas through a dedicated web service (Veale). Additional papers address in depth issues that are known to bear on the phenomenon of metaphor, such as abstractness and topicality. Dunn analyzes different kinds of abstractness and their relation to metaphoricity. Beigman Klebanov et al and Schulder and Hovy address the relationship between metaphor and topic of discussion. At the corpus level, Beigman Klebanov et al show that texts sharing a topic also share a substantial proportion of metaphors. At the level of a single text, Schulder and Hovy show that off-topic words are good candidates for metaphoricity. While previous studies and annotation efforts concentrated mostly on well-edited texts, Jang et al address social media, as well as the gap between metaphor annotations provided by trained annotators and by laypeople on a crowdsourcing website.

Complementing this diverse technical program, the workshop also features two invited talks. Dr. Brad Pasanek, an Assistant Professor in the English department at the University of Virginia, begins the talks at this year's workshop. Dr. Pasanek has collected, curated and analyzed a large collection of metaphors of mind used in 18th century British poetry; his book on the subject is forthcoming from Johns Hopkins University Press. His quantitative analysis of metaphor use by various authors provides a historical perspective on the notions of conventionality, novelty, and change in metaphor. In the neoclassical poetic tradition, the main virtue of a metaphor was not a strikingly fresh and original turn of thought (a property that is often stereotypically associated with poetic metaphor), but rather its ability to express a common thought in a particularly apt fashion ("what oft was thought, but ne'er so well expressed", to quote Alexander Pope). The idea of metaphors being in alignment with common ways of thinking while at the same time being noticeably different expressions of these thoughts has a complex and interesting relationship with the contemporary theories of conceptual metaphor.

Dr. Rebecca Resnik, Director of Mindwell Psychology Bethesda, completes the talks at this year's workshop. Dr. Resnik is a Licensed Psychologist in private practice, specializing in neuropsychological and emotional assessment of children and adults, as well as psychotherapy. The way people describe their experiences represents a pattern recognition task for clinicians, one that is at times enshrined in assessment tools (e.g., the Vanderbilt scale that asks if a child appears to be "driven by a motor"). The use of metaphor, for instance in identifying cognitive distortions and automatic negative thoughts, holds much interest for the clinical community. In exploring the relationship between metaphor and clinical diagnosis, Dr. Resnik offers a unique outlook on potential applications of metaphor-related technology.

Adjourning the workshop, a panel discussion is held to help elucidate the goals and directions of further research on metaphor in NLP. Panelists include Prof. Jerry Hobbs, University of Southern California and Dr. Tony Veale, University College Dublin.

We wish to thank everyone who showed interest and submitted a paper, all of the authors for their contributions, the members of the Program Committee for their thoughtful reviews, the invited speaker and panelists for sharing their perspectives on the topic, and all the attendees of the workshop. All of these factors contribute to a truly enriching event!

Workshop co-chairs:
Beata Beigman Klebanov, Educational Testing Service, USA
Ekaterina Shutova, University of California at Berkeley, USA
Patricia Lichtenstein, University of California at Merced, USA

Organizers:

Beata Beigman Klebanov, Educational Testing Service, USA
Ekaterina Shutova, University of California at Berkeley, USA
Patricia Lichtenstein, University of California at Merced, USA

Program Committee:

Yulia Badryzlova, Urals State Pedagogical University, Russia
John Barnden, University of Birmingham, UK
Danushka Bollegala, University of Tokyo, Japan
Ted Briscoe, University of Cambridge, UK
Stephen Clark, University of Cambridge, UK
Paul Cook, University of Melbourne, Australia
Gerard de Melo, University of California at Berkeley, USA
Jonathan Dunn, Illinois Institute of Technology, USA
Anna Feldman, Montclair State University, USA
Jerry Feldman, University of California at Berkeley, USA
Michael Flor, Educational Testing Service, USA
Yanfen Hao, Electronics Industry Research Institute, China
Eduard Hovy, Carnegie Mellon University, USA
Alexander Koller, University of Potsdam, Germany
Valia Kordoni, Humboldt University, Germany
Mark Lee, University of Birmingham, UK
Annie Louis, University of Edinburgh, UK
Katja Markert, University of Leeds, UK
James H. Martin, University of Colorado at Boulder, USA
Yusuke Miyao, National Institute of Informatics, Japan
Saif Mohammad, National Research Council Canada, Canada
Behrang Mohit, Carnegie Mellon University in Qatar, Qatar
Preslav Nakov, University of California at Berkeley, USA
Srini Narayanan, University of California at Berkeley, USA
Ani Nenkova, University of Pennsylvania, USA
Yair Neuman, Ben-Gurion University of the Negev, Israel
Malvina Nissim, University of Bologna, Italy
Thierry Poibeau, Ecole Normale Superieure and CNRS, France
Antonio Reyes, Instituto Superior de Iterpretes y Traductores, Mexico
Paolo Rosso, Universidad Politécnica de Valencia, Spain
Eyal Sagi, Northwestern University, USA
Sabine Schulte im Walde, Stuttgart University, Germany
Diarmuid Ó Séaghdha, University of Cambridge, UK
Caroline Sporleder, Saarland University, Germany
Mark Steedman, University of Edinburgh, UK
Gerard Steen, VU University of Amsterdam, The Netherlands
Mark Stevenson, University of Sheffield, UK
Carlo Strapparava, Fondazione Bruno Kessler, Italy
Tomek Strzalkowski, State University of New York at Albany, USA
Marc Tomlinson, LCC, USA
Oren Tsur, Hebrew University, Israel
Peter Turney, National Research Council Canada, Canada
Tony Veale, University College Dublin, Ireland
Aline Villavicencio, Federal University of Rio Grande do Sul, Brazil and MIT, USA

Andreas Vlachos, University of Cambridge, UK
Janyce Wiebe, University of Pittsburgh, USA

Invited Speakers:

Brad Pasanek, University of Virginia, USA
Rebecca Resnik, Mindwell Psychology, USA

Panelists:

Jerry Hobbs, University of Southern California, USA
Tony Veale, University College Dublin, Ireland

Table of Contents

Conference Program

Thursday, June 26, 2014

9:00–9:05 Opening Remarks

9:05–10:00 Invited talk: Brad Pasanek "Giving Back the Image of the Mind: Computational Approaches to 'Propriety' in Eighteenth-Century British Literature"

10:00–10:30 *Conversational Metaphors in Use: Exploring the Contrast between Technical and Everyday Notions of Metaphor*
Hyeju Jang, Mario Piergallini, Miaomiao Wen and Carolyn Rose

10:30–11:00 Coffee Break

11:00–11:30 *Different Texts, Same Metaphors: Unigrams and Beyond*
Beata Beigman Klebanov, Chee Wee Leong, Michael Heilman and Michael Flor

11:30–12:00 *Metaphor Detection through Term Relevance*
Marc Schulder and Eduard Hovy

12:00–12:30 *Multi-dimensional abstractness in cross-domain mappings*
Jonathan Dunn

Thursday, June 26, 2014 (continued)

12:30–14:00 Lunch

14:00–14:30 *Abductive Inference for Interpretation of Metaphors*
Ekaterina Ovchinnikova, Ross Israel, Suzanne Wertheim, Vladimir Zaytsev, Niloofar Montazeri and Jerry Hobbs

14:30–15:00 *Computing Affect in Metaphors*
Tomek Strzalkowski, Samira Shaikh, Kit Cho, George Aaron Broadwell, Laurie Feldman, Sarah Taylor, Boris Yamrom, Ting Liu, Ignacio Cases, Yuliya Peshkova and Kyle Elliot

15:00–15:30 *A Service-Oriented Architecture for Metaphor Processing*
Tony Veale

15:30–15:45 Coffee Break

15:45–16:30 Invited talk: Rebecca Resnik "Pandora's Box: Uses of metaphor in clinical psychology and computational linguistics"

16:30–17:30 Panel discussion: "Metaphors We Work On: Goals, Trajectories and Applications"

Conversational Metaphors in Use: Exploring the Contrast between Technical and Everyday Notions of Metaphor

Hyeju Jang, Mario Piergallini, Miaomiao Wen, and Carolyn Penstein Rosé
Language Technologies Institute
Carnegie Mellon University
Pittsburgh, PA 15213, USA
{hyejuj, mpiergal, mwen, cprose}@cs.cmu.edu

Abstract

Much computational work has been done on identifying and interpreting the meaning of metaphors, but little work has been done on understanding the motivation behind the use of metaphor. To computationally model discourse and social positioning in metaphor, we need a corpus annotated with metaphors relevant to speaker intentions. This paper reports a corpus study as a first step towards computational work on social and discourse functions of metaphor. We use Amazon Mechanical Turk (MTurk) to annotate data from three web discussion forums covering distinct domains. We then compare these to annotations from our own annotation scheme which distinguish levels of metaphor with the labels: *nonliteral*, *conventionalized*, and *literal*. Our hope is that this work raises questions about what new work needs to be done in order to address the question of how metaphors are used to achieve social goals in interaction.

1 Introduction

Our goal is to understand and characterize the ways that nonliteral language, especially metaphors, play a role in a variety of conversational strategies. In contrast to the large body of work on uncovering the intended propositional meaning behind metaphorical expressions, we are most interested in the illocutionary and perlocutionary force of the same contributions.

People use metaphorical expressions in a variety of ways in order to position themselves socially and express attitudes, as well as to make their point more effective, attractive, and convincing. Metaphors can be used to describe unfamiliar situations and feelings when the speaker feels that literal description is inadequate. They can also be used to display the speaker's creativity and wit. They can further be used as a tactic for persuasion or manipulation by foregrounding aspects that would not ordinarily be relevant. Cameron (2007) shows that we can understand social interactions and their contexts better by closely looking at these patterns of metaphor use.

Metaphors can vary in how conventionalized they are, from those which have lost their original concrete meanings to completely novel and vivid metaphors. Intuitively, it also makes sense that metaphors which are more conventional and less obviously metaphorical will be used with less conscious thought than more novel or vivid metaphors. There are thus reasons to suspect that distinguishing between levels of metaphoricity could give insight into patterns of use.

In this paper, we are interested in where we can draw a line between levels of metaphoricity. As a first step towards our long-term goal, we present a corpus study in three web discussion forums including a breast cancer support group, a Massive Open Online Course (MOOC), and a forum for street gang members, which cover distinctly different domains and have differing community structure. First, we investigate how laypeople intuitively recognize metaphor by conducting Amazon Mechanical Turk (MTurk) experiments. Second, we introduce a new annotation scheme for metaphorical expressions. In our annotation scheme, we try to map the metaphor spectrum of nonliteralness to three types of language: *nonliteral*, *conventionalized*, and *literal*. Our hope is that this distinction provides some benefit in examining the social and discourse functions of metaphor. Next, we compare MTurk

Proceedings of the Second Workshop on Metaphor in NLP, pages 1–10,
Baltimore, MD, USA, 26 June 2014. ©2014 Association for Computational Linguistics

results with our annotations. Different people will place the dividing line between literal language and metaphorical language in different places. In this work we have the opportunity to gauge how much everyday conceptions of metaphoricity diverge from theoretical perspectives and therefore how much models of metaphoricity may need to be adapted in order to adequately characterize metaphors in strategic use.

The paper is organized as follows. Section 2 relates our work to prior work on annotation and a corpus study. Section 3 describes the data used for annotation. Section 4 illustrates the functions metaphor serves in discourse through a qualitative analysis of our data. Section 5 explains our annotation scheme. Section 6 presents our annotation and MTurk experiments. Section 7 discusses the results. Section 8 concludes the paper.

2 Relation to Prior Work

In this section, we introduce the two main bodies of relevant prior work on metaphor in language technologies: computational metaphor processing and metaphor annotation.

2.1 Computational Work on Metaphor

Much of of the computational work on metaphor can be classified into two tasks: automatic identification and interpretation of metaphors.

Metaphor identification has been done using different approaches: violation of selectional preferences (Fass, 1991), linguistic cues (Goatly, 1997), source and target domain words (Stefanowitsch and Gries, 2006), clustering (Birke and Sarkar, 2006; Shutova et al., 2010), and lexical relations in WordNet (Krishnakumaran and Zhu, 2007). Gedigian et al. (2006) and Li and Sporleder (2010) distinguished the literal and nonliteral use of a target expression in text. In addition, Mason (2004) performed source-target domain mappings.

Metaphor interpretation is another large part of the computational work on metaphor. Starting with Martin (1990), a number of researchers including Narayanan (1999), Barnden and Lee (2002), Agerri et al. (2007), and Shutova (2010) have worked on the task. Metaphor identification and interpretation was performed simultaneously in (Shutova, 2013; Shutova et al., 2013b).

As we have seen so far, much of the computation work has focused on detecting and uncovering the intended meaning behind metaphorical expressions. On the other hand, Klebanov and Flor (2013) paid attention to motivations behind metaphor use, specifically metaphors used for argumentation in essays. They showed a moderate-to-strong correlation between percentage of metaphorically used words in an essay and the writing quality score. We will introduce their annotation protocol in Section 2.2.

However, to the best of our knowledge, not much computational work has been done on understanding the motivation behind the use of metaphor besides that of Klebanov and Flor (2013). Our work hopefully lays additional foundation for the needed computational work.

2.2 Metaphor Annotation

One of the main challenges in computational work on metaphor is the lack of annotated datasets. Annotating metaphorical language is nontrivial because of a lack of consensus regarding annotation schemes and clear definitions. In this section, we introduce some work dedicated to metaphor annotation and a corpus study.

Wallington et al. (2003) conducted experiments to investigate what identifies metaphors. Two different teams annotated the same text with different instructions, one asked to label "interesting stretches" and the other "metaphorical stretches". They also asked annotators to tag words or phrases that indicated a metaphor nearby, in order to investigate signals of metaphoricity.

Pragglejaz Group (2007) presented a metaphor annotation scheme, called the Metaphor Identification Procedure (MIP), which introduced a systematic approach with clear decision rules. In this scheme, a word is considered to be metaphorical if it is not used according to its most basic concrete meaning, and if its contextual meaning can be understood in comparison with the most basic concrete meaning. This method is relatively straightforward and can give high inter-reliability. Depending on how one decides upon the basic meaning of words, this scheme can be used for different applications. However, defining the basic meaning of a word is nontrivial, and following the definition of basic meaning introduced in the paper tends to result in a large proportion of words being annotated as metaphor. Many of the annotated words would not be considered to be metaphors by a layperson due to their long and widespread usage.

Later works by Steen (2010), Shutova and Teufel (2010), and Shutova et al. (2013a) expanded upon MIP. Steen (2010) discussed the strengths and weaknesses of MIP, and introduced the Metaphor Identification Procedure VU University Amsterdam (MIPVU). Shutova and Teufel (2010) and and Shutova et al. (2013a) added a procedure for identifying underlying conceptual mappings between source and target domains.

So far, these presented schemes do not distinguish between degrees of metaphoricity, and were not specifically designed for considering motivations behind metaphor use. Unlike the annotation schemes described above, Klebanov and Flor (2013) built a metaphor annotation protocol for metaphors relevant to arguments in essays. They were interested in identifying metaphors that stand out and are used to support the writer's argument. Instead of giving a formal definition of a literal sense, the annotators were instructed to mark words they thought were used metaphorically, and to write down the point being made by the metaphor, given a general definition of metaphor and examples. Our work is similar to this work in that both corpus studies pay attention to motivations behind metaphor use. However, our work focuses on more conversational discussion data whereas they focused on essays, which are more well-formed.

3 Data

We conducted experiments using data from three different web forums including a Massive Open Online Course (MOOC), a breast cancer support group (Breastcancer), and a forum for street gang members (Gang). We randomly sampled 21 posts (100 sentences) from MOOC, 8 posts (103 sentences) from Breastcancer and 44 posts (111 sentences) from Gang.

We chose these three forums because they all offer conversational data and they all differ in terms of the social situation. The forums differ significantly in purpose, demographics and the participation trajectory of members. Therefore, we expect that people will use language differently in the three sets, especially related to metaphorical expressions.

MOOC: This forum is used primarily for task-based reasons rather than socializing. People participate in the forum for a course, and leave when the course ends. As a result, the forum does not have continuity over time; participants do not spend long time with the same people.

Breastcancer: People join this forum for both task-based and social reasons: to receive informational and emotional support. People participate in the forum after they are diagnosed with cancer, and may leave the forum when they recover. This forum is also used episodically by many users, but a small percentage of users stay for long periods of time (2 or more years). Thus, continuity allows shared norms to develop over years centered around an intense shared experience.

Gang: In this forum, members belong to a distinct subculture prior to joining, whereas Breastcancer and MOOC members have less shared identity before entering the forum. This forum is purely social. There is no clear endpoint for participation; members leave the forum whenever they are not interested in it any more. Users may stay for a week or two, or for years.

4 Qualitative Analysis

Metaphors can be used for a number of conversational purposes such as increasing or decreasing social distance or as a tactic of persuasion or manipulation (Ritchie, 2013). In this section, we perform a qualitative analysis on how metaphor functions in our data. We illustrate some examples from each domain with an analysis of how some functions of social positioning are observed.

The choice of metaphor may reflect something about the attitude of the speaker. For example, *journey* is a metaphor frequently used in the breast cancer support discussion forum[1] as seen in examples (2) – (5) from the Breastcancer forum. People compare chemotherapy to a *journey* by using metaphors such as *journey*, *road* and *moves along*. A *journey* has a beginning and a goal one travels towards, but people may take different paths.

[1] http:breastcancer.org

This conveys the experience of cancer treatment as a process of progressing along a path, struggling and learning, but allows for each person's experience to differ without judgment of personal success or failure (Reisfield and Wilson, 2004). By contrast, another common metaphor compares cancer treatment to battles and war. This metaphor instead conveys an activity rather than passivity, a struggle against a defined foe, which can be won if one fights hard enough. But it also creates negative connotations for some patients, as forgoing treatment could then be seen as equivalent to surrender (ibid.).

(1) Hello Ladies! I was supposed to start chemo in January, ... I cant start tx until that is done. So I will be *joining you on your journey* this month. I AM SICK OF the ANXIETY and WAITING.

(2) So Ladies, please add another member to this club. Looks like we well all be *leaning on* each other. But I promise to *pick you up* if you *fall* if you can *catch* me once in a while!

(3) The *road* seems long now but it really *moves along* fast.

(4) I split *this journey* into 4 stages and I only deal with one.

In addition, using metaphors can have an effect of increasing empathetic understanding between the participants (Ritchie, 2013). We can see this in examples (1) – (4), where participants in the same thread use similar metaphors relating chemotherapy to a *journey*. Reusing each other's metaphors reduces emotional distance and helps to build empathic understanding and bonding through a shared perception of their situations.

Metaphor also serves to suggest associations between things that one would not normally associate. Example (5) from the MOOC forum frames participation in discussions as stepping into an arena, which refers to an area for sports or competition. By making such an analogy, it conveys an environment of direct competition in front of a large audience. It suggests that a student may be afraid of contributing to discussion because they may make a wrong statement or weak argument and another person could counter their contributions, and they will be embarrassed in front of their classmates.

(5) Hi, Vicki, great *point* – I do wish that teachers in my growing up years had been better facilitators of discussion that allowed EVERYone to practice adn become skillful at speaking...I think in the early years some of us need some *handholding* in *stepping into the arena* and speaking

Metaphors can also be used simply as a form of wordplay, to display one's wit and creativity. This can be seen in the exchange in examples (6) – (8), from the Gang forum. A common metaphor used on that forum is to refer to someone as *food* to mean that they are weak and unthreatening. The writer in (6) expands on this metaphor to suggest that the other person is especially weak by calling him *dessert*, while the writer in (7) then challenges him to fight by exploiting the meaning of *hungry* as "having a desire for *food*". The first writer (8) then dismisses him as not worth the effort to fight, as he does not *eat vegetables*.

(6) So If She Is *Food* That Must Make U *Desert*

(7) if u *hungry* nigga why wait?

(8) I Dont *Eat Vegatables*.

5 Our Annotation Scheme

When we performed qualitative analysis as in Section 4, we found that more noticeable metaphors such as "journey", "pick you up", and "fall" in (1) and (2) seem more indicative of speaker attitude or positioning than metaphors such as "point" in (5). This might suggest the degree of metaphoricity affects how metaphors function in discourse. In this section, we describe our metaphor annotation scheme, which tries to map this variation among metaphors to a simpler three-point scale of nonliteralness: *nonliteral*, *conventionalized*, and *literal*.

5.1 Basic Conditions

Our annotation scheme targets language satisfying the following three conditions:

1. the expression needs to have an original established meaning.
2. the expression needs to be used in context to mean something significantly different from that original meaning.
3. the difference in meaning should not be hyperbole, understatement, sarcasm or metonymy

These conditions result in metaphorical expressions including simile and metaphorical idioms. We consider simile to be a special case of metaphor which makes an explicit comparison using words such as "like". We include metaphorical idioms because they are obviously nonliteral and metaphorical despite the fact that they have lost their source domains.

Have an original meaning: The expression or the words within the expression need to have original established meanings. For example, in the sentence "I will be joining you on your journey this month" of (1) in Section 4, the word "journey" refers to chemotherapy given the context, but has a clear and commonly known original meaning of a physical journey from one place to another.

Alter the original and established meanings of the words: The usage needs to change the original meaning of the expression in some way. The intended meaning should be understood through a comparison to the original meaning. For the same example, in "I will be joining you on your journey this month", the intended meaning can be understood through a comparison to some characteristics of a long voyage. For metaphorical idioms such as "he kicked the bucket," the nonliteral meaning of "he died" is far from the literal meaning of "he struck the bucket with his foot."

Should not merely be hyperbole, understatement, sarcasm, or metonymy: To reduce the scope of our work, the usage needs to alter the original meaning of the expression but should not simply be a change in the intensity or the polarity of the meaning, nor should it be metonymy. Language uses like hyperbole and understatement may simply change the intensity of the meaning without otherwise altering it. For sarcasm, the intended meaning is simply the negation of the words used. Metonymy is a reference by association rather than a comparison. For example, in "The White House denied the rumor", the White House stands in for the president because it is associated with him, rather than because it is being compared to him. Note that metaphorical expressions used in conjunction with these techniques will still be coded as metaphor.

5.2 Decision Steps

To apply the basic conditions to the actual annotation procedure, we come up with a set of decision questions (Table 1). The questions rely on a variety of other syntactic and semantic distinctions serving as filtering questions. An annotator follows the questions in order after picking a phrase or word in a sentence he or she thinks might be nonliteral language. We describe some of our decisions below.

Unit: The text annotators think might be nonliteral is considered for annotation. We allow a word, a phrase, a clause, or a sentence as the unit for annotation as in (Wallington et al., 2003). We request that annotators include as few words as necessary to cover each metaphorical phrase within a sentence.

Category: We request that annotators code a candidate unit as *nonliteral*, *conventionalized*, or *literal*. We intend the *nonliteral* category to include nonliteral language usage within our scope, namely metaphors, similes, and metaphorical idioms. The *conventionalized* category is intended to cover the cases where the nonliteralness of the expression is unclear because of its extensive usage. The *literal* category is assigned to words that are literal without any doubt.

Syntactic forms: We do not include prepositions or light verbs. We do not consider phrases that consist of only function words such as modals, auxiliaries, prepositions/particles or infinitive markers. We restrict the candidate metaphorical expressions to those which contain content words.

Semantic forms: We do not include single compound words, conventional terms of address, greeting or parting phrases, or discourse markers such as "well". We also do not include terminology or jargon specific to the domain being annotated such as "twilight sedation" in healthcare, since this may be simply borrowing others' words.

No.	Question	Decision
1	Is the expression using the primary or most concrete meanings of the words?	Yes = L
2	Does the expression include a light verb that can be omitted without changing the meaning, as in "I take a shower" → "I shower"? If so, the light verb expression as a whole is literal.	Yes = L
3	Is the metaphor composed of a single compound word, like "painkiller", used in its usual meaning?	Yes = L
4	Is the expression a conventional term of address, greeting, parting phrase or a discourse marker?	Yes = L
5	Is the expression using terminology or jargon very common in this domain or medium?	Yes = L
6	Is the expression merely hyperbole/understatement, sarcasm or metonymy?	Yes = L
7	Is the expression a fixed idiom like "kick the bucket" that could have a very different concrete meaning?	Yes = N
8	Is the expression a simile, using "like" or "as" to make a comparison between unlike things?	Yes = N
9	Is the expression unconventional/creative and also using non-concrete meanings?	Yes = N
10	Is there another common way to say it that would convey all the same nuances (emotional, etc.)? Or, is this expression one of the only conventional ways of conveying that meaning?	If yes to the latter = C
11	If you cannot otherwise make a decision between literal and nonliteral, just mark it as C.	

Table 1: Questions to annotate (N: Nonliteral, C: Conventionalized, L: Literal).

6 Experiment

In this section, we present our comparative study of the MTurk annotations and the annotations based on our annotation scheme. The purpose of this experiment is to explore (1) how laypeople perceive metaphor, (2) how valid the annotations from crowdsourcing can be, and (3) how metaphors are different in the three different domains.

6.1 Experiment Setup

We had two annotators who were graduate students with some linguistic knowledge. Both were native speakers of English. The annotators were asked to annotate the data using our annotation scheme. We will call the annotators *trained annotators* from now on.

In addition, we used Amazon's Mechanical Turk (MTurk) crowdsourcing marketplace to collect laypeople's recognition of metaphors. We employed MTurk workers to annotate each sentence with the metaphorical expressions. Each sentence was given along with the full post it came from. MTurkers were instructed to copy and paste all the metaphors appearing in the sentence to given text boxes. They were given a simple definition of metaphor from Wikipedia along with a few examples to guide them. Each sentence was labeled by seven different MTurk workers, and we paid $0.05 for annotating each sentence. To control annotation quality, we required that all workers have a United States location and have 98% or more of their previous submissions accepted. We monitored the annotation job and manually filtered out annotators who submitted uniform or seemingly random annotations.

6.2 Results

To evaluate the reliability of the annotations, we used weighted Kappa (Cohen, 1968) at the word level, excluding stop words. The weighted Kappa value for annotations following our annotation scheme was 0.52, and the percent agreement was 95.68%. To measure inter-reliability between two annotators per class, we used Cohen's Kappa (Cohen, 1960). Table 2 shows the Kappa values for each dataset and each class. Table 4 shows the corpus statistics.

Dataset	N	C	N+C	Weighted
all	0.44	0.20	0.49	0.52
breastcancer	0.69	0.20	0.63	0.71
Gang	0.26	0.28	0.39	0.34
MOOC	0.41	0.13	0.47	0.53

Table 2: Inter-reliability between two trained annotators for our annotation scheme.

To evaluate the reliability of the annotations by MTurkers, we calculated Fleiss's kappa (Fleiss, 1971). Fleiss's kappa is appropriate for assessing inter-reliability when different items are rated by different judges. We measured the agreement at the word level, excluding stop words as in computing the agreement between trained annotators. The annotation was 1 if the MTurker coded a word as a metaphorical use, otherwise the annotation was 0. The Kappa values are listed in Table 3.

Dataset	Fleiss's Kappa
all	0.36
breastcancer	0.41
Gang	0.35
MOOC	0.30

Table 3: Inter-reliability among MTurkers.

We also measured the agreement between the annotations based on our scheme and MTurk annotations to see how they agree with each other. First, we made a gold standard after discussing the annotations of trained annotators. Then, to combine the seven MTurk annotations, we give a score for an expression 1 if the majority of MTurkers coded it as metaphorically used, otherwise the score is 0. Then, we computed Kappa value between trained annotators and MTurkers. The agreement between trained annotators and MTurkers was 0.51 for N and 0.40 for N + C. We can see the agreement between trained annotators and MTurkers is not that bad especially for N.

Figure 1 shows the percentage of words labeled as N, C or L according to the number of MTurkers who annotated the word as metaphorical. As seen, the more MTurkers who annotated a word, the more likely it was to be annotated as N or C by our trained annotators. The distinction between Nonliteral and Conventionalized, however, is a bit muddier, although it displays a moderate trend towards more disagreement between MTurkers for the Conventionalized category. The vast majority of words (>90%) were considered to be literal, so the sample size for comparing the N and C categories is small.

Dataset	N	N+ C
all	0.51	0.40
breastcancer	0.64	0.47
Gang	0.36	0.39
MOOC	0.65	0.36

Table 5: Inter-reliability between trained annotators and MTurkers.

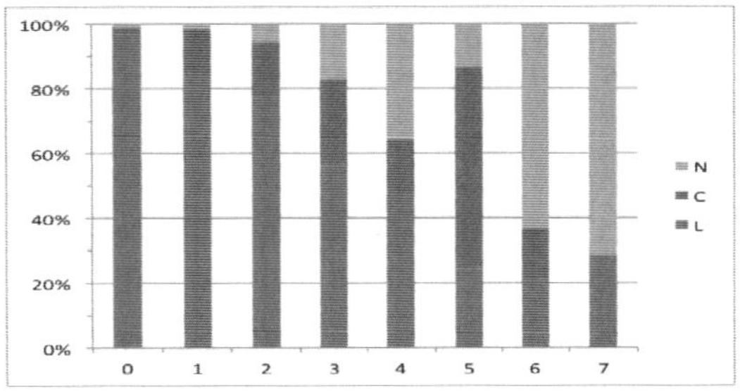

Figure 1: Correspondence between MTurkers and trained annotators. X-axis: the number of MTuckers annotating a word as metaphor.

7 Discussion

In this section, we investigate the disagreements between annotators. A problem inherent to the annotation of metaphor is that the boundary between literal and nonliteral language is fuzzy. Different annotators may draw the line in different places even when it comes to phrases they are all familiar with. It is also true that each person will have a different life history, and so some phrases which are uninteresting to one person will be strikingly metaphorical to another. For example, someone who is unfamiliar with the internet will likely find the phrase "surf the web" quite metaphorical.

Since we did not predefine the words or phrases that annotators could consider, there were often cases where one person would annotate just the

Dataset	Posts	Sent.	Words	Content Words	N	C	N/Sent.	C/Sent.
MOOC	21	100	2005	982	23	59	0.23	0.59
Breastcancer	8	103	1598	797	27	41	0.26	0.4
Gang	44	111	1403	519	30	51	0.27	0.46

Table 4: Data statistics.

noun and another might include the entire noun phrase. If it was part of a conventional multi-word expression, MTurkers seemed likely to include the entire collocation, not merely the metaphorical part. Boundaries were an issue to a lesser extent with our trained annotators.

One of our datasets, the Gang forum, uses a lot of slang and non-standard grammar and spellings. One of our trained annotators is quite familiar with this forum and the other is not. This was the set they had the most disagreement on. For example, the one annotator did not recognize names of certain gangs and rap musicians, and thought they were meant metaphorically. Similarly, the MTurkers had trouble with many of the slang expressions in this data.

Another issue for the MTurkers is the distinction between metaphor and other forms of nonliteral language such as metonymy and hyperbole. For example, in the Gang data, the term "ass" is used to refer to a whole person. This is a type metonymy (synecdoche) using a part to refer to the whole. MTurkers were likely to label such expressions as metaphor. Hyperbolic expressions like "never in a million years" were also marked by some MTurkers.

In a few cases, the sentence may have required more context to decipher, such as previous posts in the same thread. Another minor issue was that some data had words misspelled as other words or grammatical errors, which some MTurkers annotated as metaphors.

Certain categories of conventionalized metaphors that would be annotated in the original presentation of MIP (Pragglejaz-Group, 2007) were never or almost never annotated by MTurkers. These included light verbs such as "make" or "get" when used as causatives or the passive "get", verbs of sensation used for cognitive meanings, such as "see" meaning "understand", and demonstratives and prepositions in themselves. This may indicate something about the relevance of these types of metaphors for certain applications.

8 Conclusion

We annotated data from three distinct conversational online forums using both MTurks and our annotation scheme. The comparison between these two annotations revealed a few things. One is that MTurkers did not show high agreement among themselves, but showed acceptable agreement with trained annotators for the N category. Another is that domain-specific knowledge is important for accurate identification of metaphors. Even trained annotators will have difficulty if they are not familiar with the domain because they may not even understand the meaning of the language used.

Our annotation scheme has room for improvement. For example, we need to distinguish between the Conventionalized and Nonliteral categories more clearly. We will refine the coding scheme further as we work with more annotators.

We also think there may be methods of processing MTurk annotations to improve their correspondence with annotations based on our coding scheme. This could address issues such as inconsistent phrase boundaries or distinguishing between metonymy and metaphor. This could make it possible to use crowdsourcing to annotate the larger amounts of data required for computational applications in a reasonable amount of time.

Our research is in the beginning phase working towards the goal of computational modeling of social and discourse uses of metaphor. Our next steps in that direction will be to work on developing our annotated dataset and then begin to investigate the differing contexts that metaphors are used in. Our eventual goal is to be able to apply computational methods to interpret metaphor at the level of social positioning and discourse functions.

Acknowledgments

This work was supported by NSF grant IIS-1302522, and Army research lab grant W911NF-11-2-0042.

References

Rodrigo Agerri, John Barnden, Mark Lee, and Alan Wallington. 2007. Metaphor, inference and domain independent mappings. In *Proceedings of RANLP*, pages 17–23. Citeseer.

John A Barnden and Mark G Lee. 2002. An artificial intelligence approach to metaphor understanding. *Theoria et Historia Scientiarum*, 6(1):399–412.

Julia Birke and Anoop Sarkar. 2006. A clustering approach for nearly unsupervised recognition of nonliteral language. In *EACL*.

Lynne J Cameron. 2007. Patterns of metaphor use in reconciliation talk. *Discourse & Society*, 18(2):197–222.

J. Cohen. 1960. A coefficient of agreement for nominal scales. *Educational and Psychological Measurement*, 20:37–46.

Jacob Cohen. 1968. Weighted kappa: Nominal scale agreement provision for scaled disagreement or partial credit. *Psychological bulletin*, 70(4):213.

Dan Fass. 1991. met*: A method for discriminating metonymy and metaphor by computer. *Computational Linguistics*, 17(1):49–90.

Joseph L Fleiss. 1971. Measuring nominal scale agreement among many raters. *Psychological bulletin*, 76(5):378–382.

Matt Gedigian, John Bryant, Srini Narayanan, and Branimir Ciric. 2006. Catching metaphors. In *Proceedings of the Third Workshop on Scalable Natural Language Understanding*, pages 41–48. Association for Computational Linguistics.

Andrew Goatly. 1997. *Language of Metaphors: Literal Metaphorical.* Routledge.

Beata Beigman Klebanov and Michael Flor. 2013. Argumentation-relevant metaphors in test-taker essays. *Meta4NLP 2013*, pages 11–20.

Saisuresh Krishnakumaran and Xiaojin Zhu. 2007. Hunting elusive metaphors using lexical resources. In *Proceedings of the Workshop on Computational approaches to Figurative Language*, pages 13–20. Association for Computational Linguistics.

Linlin Li and Caroline Sporleder. 2010. Using gaussian mixture models to detect figurative language in context. In *Human Language Technologies: The 2010 Annual Conference of the North American Chapter of the Association for Computational Linguistics*, HLT '10, pages 297–300, Stroudsburg, PA, USA. Association for Computational Linguistics.

James H Martin. 1990. *A computational model of metaphor interpretation.* Academic Press Professional, Inc.

Zachary J Mason. 2004. Cormet: a computational, corpus-based conventional metaphor extraction system. *Computational Linguistics*, 30(1):23–44.

Srinivas Narayanan. 1999. Moving right along: A computational model of metaphoric reasoning about events. In *AAAI/IAAI*, pages 121–127.

Pragglejaz-Group. 2007. Mip: A method for identifying metaphorically used words in discourse. *Metaphor and symbol*, 22(1):1–39.

Gary M Reisfield and George R Wilson. 2004. Use of metaphor in the discourse on cancer. *Journal of Clinical Oncology*, 22(19):4024–4027.

SL. David Ritchie. 2013. *Metaphor (Key Topics in Semantics and Pragmatics).* Cambridge university press.

Ekaterina Shutova and Simone Teufel. 2010. Metaphor corpus annotated for source-target domain mappings. In *LREC*.

Ekaterina Shutova, Lin Sun, and Anna Korhonen. 2010. Metaphor identification using verb and noun clustering. In *Proceedings of the 23rd International Conference on Computational Linguistics*, pages 1002–1010. Association for Computational Linguistics.

Ekaterina Shutova, BarryJ. Devereux, and Anna Korhonen. 2013a. Conceptual metaphor theory meets the data: a corpus-based human annotation study. *Language Resources and Evaluation*, 47(4):1261–1284.

Ekaterina Shutova, Simone Teufel, and Anna Korhonen. 2013b. Statistical metaphor processing. *Computational Linguistics*, 39(2):301–353.

Ekaterina Shutova. 2010. Automatic metaphor interpretation as a paraphrasing task. In *Human Language Technologies: The 2010 Annual Conference of the North American Chapter of the Association for Computational Linguistics*, pages 1029–1037. Association for Computational Linguistics.

Ekaterina Shutova. 2013. Metaphor identification as interpretation. *Atlanta, Georgia, USA*, page 276.

Gerard J Steen, Aletta G Dorst, J Berenike Herrmann, Anna Kaal, Tina Krennmayr, and Trijntje Pasma. 2010. *A method for linguistic metaphor identification: From MIP to MIPVU*, volume 14. John Benjamins Publishing.

Anatol Stefanowitsch and Stefan Th Gries. 2006. *Corpus-based approaches to metaphor and metonymy*, volume 171. Walter de Gruyter.

AM Wallington, JA Barnden, P Buchlovsky, L Fellows, and SR Glasbey. 2003. Metaphor annotation: A systematic study. *COGNITIVE SCIENCE RESEARCH PAPERS-UNIVERSITY OF BIRMINGHAM CSRP*.

Different Texts, Same Metaphors: Unigrams and Beyond

Beata Beigman Klebanov, Chee Wee Leong, Michael Heilman, Michael Flor
Educational Testing Service
660 Rosedale Road
Princeton, NJ 08541
{bbeigmanklebanov,cleong,mheilman,mflor}@ets.org

Abstract

Current approaches to supervised learning of metaphor tend to use sophisticated features and restrict their attention to constructions and contexts where these features apply. In this paper, we describe the development of a supervised learning system to classify all content words in a running text as either being used metaphorically or not. We start by examining the performance of a simple unigram baseline that achieves surprisingly good results for some of the datasets. We then show how the recall of the system can be improved over this strong baseline.

1 Introduction

Current approaches to supervised learning of metaphor tend to (a) use sophisticated features based on theories of metaphor, (b) apply to certain selected constructions, like adj-noun or verb-object pairs, and (c) concentrate on metaphors of certain kind, such as metaphors about governance or about the mind. In this paper, we describe the development of a supervised machine learning system to classify all content words in a running text as either being used metaphorically or not – a task not yet addressed in the literature, to our knowledge. This approach would enable, for example, quantification of the extent to which a given text uses metaphor, or the extent to which two different texts use similar metaphors. Both of these questions are important in our target application – scoring texts (in our case, essays written for a test) for various aspects of effective use of language, one of them being the use of metaphor.

We start by examining the performance of a simple unigram baseline that achieves surprisingly good results for some of the datasets. We then show how the recall of the system can be improved over this strong baseline.

2 Data

We use two datasets that feature full text annotations of metaphors: A set of essays written for a large-scale assessment of college graduates and the VUAmsterdam corpus (Steen et al., 2010),[1] containing articles from four genres sampled from the BNC. Table 1 shows the sizes of the six sets, as well as the proportion of metaphors in them; the following sections explain their composition.

Data	#Texts	#NVAR tokens	#metaphors (%)
News	49	18,519	3,405 (18%)
Fiction	11	17,836	2,497 (14%)
Academic	12	29,469	3,689 (13%)
Conversation	18	15,667	1,149 (7%)
Essay Set A	85	21,838	2,368 (11%)
Essay Set B	79	22,662	2,745 (12%)

Table 1: Datasets used in this study. NVAR = Nouns, Verbs, Adjectives, Adverbs, as tagged by the Stanford POS tagger (Toutanova et al., 2003).

2.1 VUAmsterdam Data

The dataset consists of 117 fragments sampled across four genres: Academic, News, Conversation, and Fiction. Each genre is represented by approximately the same number of tokens, although the number of texts differs greatly, where the news archive has the largest number of texts.

We randomly sampled 23% of the texts from each genre to set aside for a blind test to be carried out at a later date with a more advanced system; the current experiments are performed using cross-validation on the remaining 90 fragments: 10-fold on News, 9-fold on Conversation, 11 on Fiction, and 12 on Academic. All instances from the same text were always placed in the same fold.

[1] http://www2.let.vu.nl/oz/metaphorlab/metcor/search/index.html

Proceedings of the Second Workshop on Metaphor in NLP, pages 11–17,
Baltimore, MD, USA, 26 June 2014.

The data is annotated using MIP-VU procedure. It is based on the MIP procedure (Pragglejaz, 2007), extending it to handle metaphoricity through reference (such as marking *did* as a metaphor in *As the weather broke up, so did their friendship*) and allow for explicit coding of difficult cases where a group of annotators could not arrive at a consensus. The tagset is rich and is organized hierarchically, detecting various types of metaphors, words that flag the presense of metaphors, etc. In this paper, we consider only the top-level partition, labeling all content words with the tag "function=mrw" (metaphor-related word) as metaphors, while all other content words are labeled as non-metaphors.[2]

2.2 Essay Data

The dataset consists of 224 essays written for a high-stakes large-scale assessment of analytical writing taken by college graduates aspiring to enter a graduate school in the United States. Out of these, 80 were set aside for future experiments and not used for this paper. Of the remaining essays, 85 essays discuss the statement "High-speed electronic communications media, such as electronic mail and television, tend to prevent meaningful and thoughtful communication" (**Set A**), and 79 discuss the statement "In the age of television, reading books is not as important as it once was. People can learn as much by watching television as they can by reading books." (**Set B**). Multiple essays on the same topic is a unique feature of this dataset, allowing the examination of the effect of topic on performance, by comparing performance in within-topic and across-topic settings.

The essays were annotated using a protocol that prefers a reader's intuition over a formal definition, and emphasizes the connection between metaphor and the arguments that are put forward by the writer. The protocol is presented in detail in Beigman Klebanov and Flor (2013). All essays were doubly annotated. The reliability is $\kappa = 0.58$ for Set A and $\kappa = 0.56$ for Set B. We merge the two annotations (union), following the observation in a previous study Beigman Klebanov et al. (2008) that attention slips play a large role in accounting for observed disagreements.

We will report results for 10-fold cross-validation on each of sets A and B, as well as across prompts, where the machine learner would be trained on Set A and tested on Set B and vice versa.

3 Supervised Learning of Metaphor

For this study, we consider each content-word token in a text as an instance to be classified as a metaphor or non-metaphor. We use the logistic regression classifier in the SKLL package (Blanchard et al., 2013), which is based on scikit-learn (Pedregosa et al., 2011), optimizing for F_1 score (class "metaphor"). We consider the following features for metaphor detection.

- **Unigrams (U)**: All content words from the relevant training data are used as features, without stemming or lemmatization.
- **Part-of-Speech (P)**: We use Stanford POS tagger 3.3.0 and the full Penn Treebank tagset for content words (tags starting with A, N, V, and J), removing the auxiliaries *have, be, do*.
- **Concreteness (C)**: We use Brysbaert et al. (2013) database of concreteness ratings for about 40,000 English words. The mean ratings, ranging 1-5, are binned in 0.25 increments; each bin is used as a binary feature.
- **Topic models (T)**: We use Latent Dirichlet Allocation (Blei et al., 2003) to derive a 100-topic model from the NYT corpus years 2003–2007 (Sandhaus, 2008) to represent common topics of public discussion. The NYT data was lemmatized using NLTK (Bird, 2006). We used the gensim toolkit (Řehůřek and Sojka, 2010) for building the models, with default parameters. The score assigned to an instance w on a topic t is $log\frac{P(w|t)}{P(w)}$ where $P(w)$ were estimated from the Gigaword corpus (Parker et al., 2009). These features are based on the hypothesis that certain topics are likelier to be used as source domains for metaphors than others.

4 Results

For each dataset, we present the results for the unigram model (**baseline**) and the results for the full model containing all the features. For cross-validation results, all words from the same text were always placed in the same fold, to ensure that we are evaluating generalization across texts.

[2] We note that this top-level partition was used for many of the analyses discussed in (Steen et al., 2010).

Data	M	Unigram			UPCT		
	F	P	R	F	P	R	F
Set A	.20	.72	.43	.53	.70	.47	.56
Set B	.22	.79	.54	.64	.76	.60	.67
B-A	.20	.58	.45	.50	.56	.50	.53
A-B	.22	.71	.28	.40	.72	.35	.47
News	.31	.62	.38	.47	.61	.43	.51
Fiction	.25	.54	.23	.32	.54	.24	.33
Acad.	.23	.51	.20	.27	.50	.22	.28
Conv.	.14	.39	.14	.21	.36	.15	.21

Table 2: Summary of performance, in terms of precision, recall, and F_1. Set A, B, and VUAmsterdam: cross-validation. B-A and A-B: Training on B and testing on A, and vice versa, respectively. Column M: F_1 of a pseudo-system that classifies all words as metaphors.

4.1 Performance of the Baseline Model

First, we observe the strong performance of the unigram baseline for the cross-validation within sets A and B (rows 1 and 2 in Table 2). For a new essay, about half its metaphors will have been observed in a sample of a few dozen essays on the same topic; these words are also consistently used as metaphors, as precision is above 70%. Once the same-topic assumption is relaxed down to related topics, the sharing of metaphor is reduced (compare rows 1 vs 3 and 2 vs 4), but still substantial.

Moving to VUAmsterdam data, we observe that the performance of the unigram model on the News partition is comparable to its performance in the cross-prompt scenario in the essay data (compare row 5 to rows 3-4 in Table 2), suggesting that the News fragments tend to discuss a set of related topics and exhibit substantial sharing of metaphors across texts.

The performance of the unigram model is much lower for the other VUAmsterdam partitions, although it is still non-trivial, as evidenced by its consistent improvement over a pseudo-baseline that classifies all words as metaphor, attaining 100% recall (shown in column M in Table 2). The weaker performance could be due to highly divergent topics between texts in each of the partitions. It is also possible that the number of different texts in these partitions is insufficient for covering the metaphors that are common in these kinds of texts – recall that these partitions have small numbers of long texts, whereas the News partition has a larger number of short texts (see Table 1).

4.2 Beyond Baseline

The addition of topic model, POS, and concreteness features produces a significant increase in recall across all evaluations ($p < 0.01$), using McNemar's test of the significance of differences between correlated proportions (McNemar, 1947). Even for Conversations, where recall improvement is the smallest and F_1 score does not improve, the UPCT model recovers all 161 metaphors found by the unigrams plus 14 additional metaphors, yielding a significant result on the correlated test.

We next investigate the relative contribution of the different types of features in the UPCT model by ablating each type and observing the effect on performance. Table 3 shows ablation results for essay and News data, where substantial improvements over the unigram baseline were produced.

We observe, as expected, that the unigram features contributed the most, as removing them results in the most dramatic drop in performance, although the combination of concreteness, POS, and topic models recovers about one-fourth of metaphors with over 50% precision, showing non-trivial performance on essay data.

The second most effective feature set for essay data are the topic models – they are responsible for most of the recall gain obtained by the UPCT model. For example, one of the topics with a positive weight in essays in set B deals with visual imagery, its top 5 most likely words in the NYT being *picture, image, photograph, camera, photo*. This topic is often used metaphorically, with words like *superficial, picture, framed, reflective, mirror, capture, vivid, distorted, exposure, scenes, face, background* that were all observed as metaphors in Set B. In the News data, a topic that deals with hurricane Katrina received a positive weight, as words of suffering and recovery from distaster are often used metaphorically when discussing other things: *starved, severed, awash, damaged, relief, victim, distress, hits, swept, bounce, response, recovering, suffering*.

The part-of-speech features help improve recall across all datasets in Table 3, while concreteness features are effective only for some of the sets.

5 Discussion: Metaphor & Word Sense

The classical "one sense per discourse" finding of Gale et al. (1992) that words keep their senses within the same text 98% of the time suggests that

	Set A cross-val.			Set B cross-val.			Train B : Test A			Train A : Test B			News		
	P	R	F	P	R	F	P	R	F	P	R	F	P	R	F
M	.11	1.0	.20	.12	1.0	.22	.11	1.0	.20	.12	1.0	.22	.18	1.0	.31
U	.72	.43	.53	.79	.54	.64	.58	.45	.50	.71	.28	.40	.62	.38	.47
UPCT	.70	.47	.56	.76	.60	.67	.56	.50	.53	.72	.35	.47	.61	.43	.51
– U	.58	.21	.31	.63	.28	.38	.44	.21	.29	.59	.18	.27	.55	.23	.32
– P	.71	.46	.56	.76	.58	.66	.57	.48	.52	.70	.33	.45	.61	.41	.49
– C	.70	.46	.55	.77	.58	.66	.56	.50	.53	.71	.34	.46	.61	.43	.50
– T	.71	.43	.53	.78	.55	.65	.57	.45	.51	.71	.29	.41	.62	.41	.49

Table 3: Ablation evaluations. Model M is a pseudo-system that classifies all instances as metaphors.

if a word is used as a metaphor once in a text, it is very likely to be a metaphor if it is used again in the same text. Indeed, this is the reason for putting all words from the same text in the same fold in cross-validations, as training and testing on different parts of the same text would produce inflated estimates of metaphor classification performance.

Koeling et al. (2005) extend the notion of discourse beyond a single text to a domain, such as articles on Finance, Sports, and a general BNC domain. For a set of words that each have at least one Finance and one Sports sense and not more than 12 senses in total, guessing the predominant sense in Finance and Sports yielded 77% and 76% precision, respectively. Our results with the unigram model show that guessing "metaphor" based on a sufficient proportion of previously observed metaphorical uses in the given domain yields about 76% precision for essays on the same topic. Thus, metaphoricity distinctions in same-topic essays behave similarly to sense distinctions for polysemous words with a predominant sense in the Finance and Sports articles, keeping to their domain-specific predominant sense $\frac{3}{4}$ of the time.

Note that a domain-specific predominant sense may or may not be the same as the most frequent sense overall; similarly, a word's tendency to be used metaphorically might be domain specific or general. The results for the BNC at large are likely to reflect general rather than domain-specific sense distributions. According to Koeling et al. (2005), guessing the predominant sense in the BNC yields 51% precision; our finding for BNC News is 62% precision for the unigram model. The difference could be due to the mixing of the BNC genres in Koeling et al. (2005), given the lower precision of metaphoricity prediction in non-news (Table 2).

In all, our results suggest that the pattern of metaphorical and non-metaphorical use is in line with that of dominant word-sense for more and less topically restricted domains.

6 Related Work

The extent to which different texts use similar metaphors was addressed by Pasanek and Sculley (2008) for corpora written by the same author. They studied metaphors of mind in the oeuvre of 7 authors, including John Milton and William Shakespeare. They created a set of metaphorical and non-metaphorical references to the mind using excerpts from various texts written by these authors. Using cross-validation with unigram features for each of the authors separately, they present very high accuracies (85%-94%), suggesting that authors are highly self-consistent in the metaphors of mind they select. They also find good generalizations between some pairs of authors, due to borrowing or literary allusion.

Studies using political texts, such as speeches by politicians or news articles discussing politically important events, documented repeated use of words from certain source domains, such as rejuvenation in Tony Blair's speeches (Charteris-Black, 2005) or railroad metaphors in articles discussing political integration of Europe (Musolff, 2000). Our results regarding settings with substantial topical consistency second these observations.

According to the Conceptual Metaphor theory (Lakoff and Johnson, 1980), we expect certain basic metaphors to be highly ubiquitous in any corpus of texts, such as TIME IS SPACE or UP IS GOOD. To the extent that these metaphors are realized through frequent content words, we expect some cross-text generalization power for a unigram model. Perhaps the share of these basic metaphors in all metaphors in a text is reflected most faithfully in the peformance of the unigram model on the non-News partitions of the VUAmsterdam data, where topical sharing is minimal.

Approaches to metaphor detection are often either rule-based or unsupervised (Martin, 1990; Fass, 1991; Shutova et al., 2010; Shutova and Sun, 2013; Li et al., 2013), although supervised approaches have recently been attempted with the advent of relatively large collections of metaphor-annotated materials (Mohler et al., 2013; Hovy et al., 2013; Pasanek and Sculley, 2008; Gedigan et al., 2006). These approaches are difficult to compare to our results, as these typically are not whole texts but excerpts, and only certain kinds of metaphors are annotated, such as metaphors about governance or about the mind, or only words belonging to certain syntactic or semantic class are annotated, such as verbs[3] or motion words only.

Concreteness as a predictor of metaphoricity was discussed in Turney et al. (2011) in the context of concrete adjectives modifying abstract nouns. The POS features are inspired by the discussion of the preference and aversion of various POS towards metaphoricity in Goatly (1997). Heintz et al. (2013) use LDA topics built on Wikipedia along with manually constructed seed lists for potential source and target topics in the broad target domain of governance, in order to identify sentences using lexica from both source and target domains as potentially containing metaphors. Bethard et al. (2009) use LDA topics built on BNC as features for classifying metaphorical and non-metaphorical uses of 9 words in 450 sentences that use these words, modeling metaphorical vs non-metaphorical contexts for these words. In both cases, LDA is used to capture the topical composition of a sentence; in contrast, we use LDA to capture the tendency of words belonging to a topic to be used metaphorically in a given discourse.

Dunn (2013) compared algorithms based on various theories of metaphor on VUAmsterdam data. The evaluations were done at sentence level, where a sentence is metaphorical if it contains at least one metaphorically used word. In this accounting, the distribution is almost a mirror-image of our setting, as 84% of sentences in News were labeled as metaphorical, whereas 18% of content words are tagged as such. The News partition was very difficult for the systems examined in Dunn (2013) – three of the four systems failed to predict any non-metaphorical sentences, and the one system that did so suffered from a low recall of metaphors, 20%. Dunn (2013) shows that the different systems he compared had relatively low agreement ($\kappa < 0.3$); he interprets this finding as suggesting that the different theories underlying the models capture different aspects of metaphoricity and therefore detect different metaphors. It is therefore likely that features derived from the various models would fruitfully complement each other in a supervised learning setting; our findings suggest that the simplest building block – that of a unigram model – should not be ignored in such experiments.

7 Conclusions

We address supervised learning of metaphoricity of words of any content part of speech in a running text. To our knowledge, this task has not yet been studied in the literature. We experimented with a simple unigram model that was surprisingly successful for some of the datasets, and showed how its recall can be further improved using topic models, POS, and concreteness features.

The generally solid performance of the unigram features suggests that these features should not be neglected when trying to predict metaphors in a supervised learning paradigm. Inasmuch as metaphoricity classification is similar to a coarse-grained word sense disambiguation, a unigram model can be thought of as a crude predominant sense model for WSD, and is the more effective the more topically homogeneous the data.

By evaluating models with LDA-based topic features in addition to unigrams, we showed that topical homogeneity can be exploited beyond unigrams. In topically homogeneous data, certain topics commonly discussed in the public sphere might not be addressed, yet their general familiarity avails them as sources for metaphors. For essays on communication, topics like sports and architecture are unlikely to be discussed; yet metaphors from these domains can be used, such as *leveling of the playing field* through cheap and fast communications or *buildling bridges* across cultures through the internet.

In future work, we intend to add features that capture the relationship between the current word and its immediate context, as well as add essays from additional prompts to build a more topically diverse set for exploration of cross-topic generalization of our models for essay data.

[3]as in Shutova and Teufel (2010)

References

Beata Beigman Klebanov and Michael Flor. 2013. Argumentation-relevant metaphors in test-taker essays. In *Proceedings of the First Workshop on Metaphor in NLP*, pages 11–20, Atlanta, Georgia, June. Association for Computational Linguistics.

Beata Beigman Klebanov, Eyal Beigman, and Daniel Diermeier. 2008. Analyzing disagreements. In *COLING 2008 workshop on Human Judgments in Computational Linguistics*, pages 2–7, Manchester, UK.

Steven Bethard, Vicky Tzuyin Lai, and James Martin. 2009. Topic model analysis of metaphor frequency for psycholinguistic stimuli. In *Proceedings of the Workshop on Computational Approaches to Linguistic Creativity*, CALC '09, pages 9–16, Stroudsburg, PA, USA. Association for Computational Linguistics.

Steven Bird. 2006. NLTK: The natural language toolkit. In *Proceedings of the ACL, Interactive Presentations*, pages 69–72.

Daniel Blanchard, Michael Heilman, and Nitin Madnani. 2013. *SciKit-Learn Laboratory*. GitHub repository, https://github.com/EducationalTestingService/skll.

David M. Blei, Andrew Y. Ng, and Michael I. Jordan. 2003. Latent Dirichlet Allocation. *Journal of Machine Learning Research*, 3:993–1022.

Marc Brysbaert, Amy Beth Warriner, and Victor Kuperman. 2013. Concreteness ratings for 40 thousand generally known english word lemmas. *Behavior Research Methods*, pages 1–8.

Jonathan Charteris-Black. 2005. *Politicians and rhetoric: The persuasive power of metaphors*. Palgrave MacMillan, Houndmills, UK and New York.

Jonathan Dunn. 2013. What metaphor identification systems can tell us about metaphor-in-language. In *Proceedings of the First Workshop on Metaphor in NLP*, pages 1–10, Atlanta, Georgia, June. Association for Computational Linguistics.

Dan Fass. 1991. Met*: A method for discriminating metonymy and metaphor by computer. *Computational Linguistics*, 17(1):49–90.

William Gale, Kenneth Church, and David Yarowsky. 1992. One sense per discourse. In *Proceedings of the Speech and Natural Language Workshop*, pages 233–237.

Matt Gedigan, John Bryant, Srini Narayanan, and Branimir Ciric. 2006. Catching metaphors. In *Proceedings of the 3rd Workshop on Scalable Natural Language Understanding*, pages 41–48, New York.

Andrew Goatly. 1997. *The Language of Metaphors*. Routledge, London.

Ilana Heintz, Ryan Gabbard, Mahesh Srivastava, Dave Barner, Donald Black, Majorie Friedman, and Ralph Weischedel. 2013. Automatic Extraction of Linguistic Metaphors with LDA Topic Modeling. In *Proceedings of the First Workshop on Metaphor in NLP*, pages 58–66, Atlanta, Georgia, June. Association for Computational Linguistics.

Dirk Hovy, Shashank Srivastava, Sujay Kumar Jauhar, Mrinmaya Sachan, Kartik Goyal, Huying Li, Whitney Sanders, and Eduard Hovy. 2013. Identifying metaphorical word use with tree kernels. In *Proceedings of the First Workshop on Metaphor in NLP*, pages 52–57, Atlanta, GA. Association for Computational Linguistics.

Rob Koeling, Diana McCarthy, and John Carroll. 2005. Domain-specific sense distributions and predominant sense acquisition. In *Proceedings of HLT-EMNLP*, pages 419–426, Vancouver, Canada. Association for Computational Linguistics.

George Lakoff and Mark Johnson. 1980. *Metaphors we live by*. University of Chicago Press, Chicago.

Hongsong Li, Kenny Q. Zhu, and Haixun Wang. 2013. Data-driven metaphor recognition and explanation. *Transactions of the ACL*, 1:379–390.

James Martin. 1990. *A computational model of metaphor interpretation*. Academic Press Professional, Inc., San Diego, CA, USA.

Quinn McNemar. 1947. Note on the sampling error of the difference between correlated proportions or percentages. *Psychometrika*, 12(2):153–157.

Michael Mohler, David Bracewell, Marc Tomlinson, and David Hinote. 2013. Semantic signatures for example-based linguistic metaphor detection. In *Proceedings of the First Workshop on Metaphor in NLP*, pages 27–35, Atlanta, GA. Association for Computational Linguistics.

Andreas Musolff. 2000. *Mirror images of Europe: Metaphors in the public debate about Europe in Britain and Germany*. München: Iudicium. Annotated data is available at http://www.dur.ac.uk/andreas.musolff/Arcindex.htm.

Robert Parker, David Graff, Junbo Kong, Ke Chen, and Kazuaki Maeda. 2009. English Gigaword Fourth Edition LDC2009T13. Linguistic Data Consortium, Philadelphia.

Bradley Pasanek and D. Sculley. 2008. Mining millions of metaphors. *Literary and Linguistic Computing*, 23(3):345–360.

Fabian Pedregosa, Gael Varoquaux, Alexandre Gramfort, Vincent Michel, Bertrand Thirion, Olivier Grisel, Mathieu Blondel, Peter Prettenhofer, Ron Weiss, Vincent Dubourg, Jake VanderPlas, Alexandre Passos, David Cournapeau, Matthieu Brucher, Matthieu Perrot, and Edouard Duchesnay. 2011. Scikit-learn: Machine learning in Python. *Journal of Machine Learning Research*, 12:2825–2830.

Group Pragglejaz. 2007. MIP: A Method for Identifying Metaphorically Used Words in Discourse. *Metaphor and Symbol*, 22(1):1–39.

Radim Řehůřek and Petr Sojka. 2010. Software Framework for Topic Modelling with Large Corpora. In *Proceedings of the LREC 2010 Workshop on New Challenges for NLP Frameworks*, pages 45–50, Valletta, Malta, May. ELRA.

Evan Sandhaus. 2008. The New York Times Annotated Corpus. LDC Catalog No: LDC2008T19.

Ekaterina Shutova and Lin Sun. 2013. Unsupervised metaphor identification using hierarchical graph factorization clustering. In *Proceedings of HLT-NAACL*, pages 978–988.

Ekaterina Shutova and Simone Teufel. 2010. Metaphor corpus annotated for source - target domain mappings. In Nicoletta Calzolari (Conference Chair), Khalid Choukri, Bente Maegaard, Joseph Mariani, Jan Odijk, Stelios Piperidis, Mike Rosner, and Daniel Tapias, editors, *Proceedings of the Seventh International Conference on Language Resources and Evaluation (LREC'10)*, pages 3255–3261, Valletta, Malta, May. European Language Resources Association (ELRA).

Ekaterina Shutova, Lin Sun, and Anna Korhonen. 2010. Metaphor identification using verb and noun clustering. In *Proceedings of the 23rd International Conference on Computational Linguistics (COLING)*, pages 1002–1010.

Gerard Steen, Aletta Dorst, Berenike Herrmann, Anna Kaal, Tina Krennmayr, and Trijntje Pasma. 2010. *A Method for Linguistic Metaphor Identification*. Amsterdam: John Benjamins.

Kristina Toutanova, Dan Klein, Christopher Manning, and Yoram Singer. 2003. Feature-Rich Part-of-Speech Tagging with a Cyclic Dependency Network. In *Proceedings of NAACL*, pages 252–259.

Peter Turney, Yair Neuman, Dan Assaf, and Yohai Cohen. 2011. Literal and metaphorical sense identification through concrete and abstract context. In *Proceedings of the Conference on Empirical Methods in Natural Language Processing*, pages 680–690, Stroudsburg, PA, USA. Association for Computational Linguistics.

Metaphor Detection through Term Relevance

Marc Schulder
Spoken Language Systems
Saarland University
Saarbrücken, Germany
marc.schulder@lsv.uni-saarland.de

Eduard Hovy
Language Technologies Institute
Carnegie Mellon University
Pittsburth, PA, USA
hovy@cs.cmu.edu

Abstract

Most computational approaches to metaphor detection try to leverage either conceptual metaphor mappings or selectional preferences. Both require extensive knowledge of the mappings/preferences in question, as well as sufficient data for all involved conceptual domains. Creating these resources is expensive and often limits the scope of these systems.

We propose a statistical approach to metaphor detection that utilizes the rarity of novel metaphors, marking words that do not match a text's typical vocabulary as metaphor candidates. No knowledge of semantic concepts or the metaphor's source domain is required.

We analyze the performance of this approach as a stand-alone classifier and as a feature in a machine learning model, reporting improvements in F_1 measure over a random baseline of 58% and 68%, respectively. We also observe that, as a feature, it appears to be particularly useful when data is sparse, while its effect diminishes as the amount of training data increases.

1 Introduction

Metaphors are used to replace complicated or unfamiliar ideas with familiar, yet unrelated concepts that share an important attribute with the intended idea. In NLP, detecting metaphors and other nonliteral figures of speech is necessary to interpret their meaning correctly. As metaphors are a productive part of language, listing known examples is not sufficient. Most computational approaches to metaphor detection are based either on the theory of conceptual mappings (Lakoff and Johnson, 1980) or that of preference violation (Wilks, 1978).

Lakoff and Johnson (1980) showed that metaphors have underlying mappings between two conceptual domains: The figurative *source* domain that the metaphor is taken from and the literal *target* domain of the surrounding context in which it has to be interpreted. Various metaphors can be based on the same conceptual metaphor mapping, e.g. both *"The economy is a* ***house of cards****"* and *"the* ***stakes*** *of our debates appear small"* match POLITICS IS A GAME.

Another attribute of metaphors is that they violate semantic *selectional preferences* (Wilks, 1978). The theory of selectional preference observes that verbs constrain their syntactic arguments by the semantic concepts they accept in these positions. Metaphors violate these constraints, combining incompatible concepts.

To make use of these theories, extensive knowledge of pairings (either mappings or preferences) and the involved conceptual domains is required. Especially in the case of conceptual mappings, this makes it very difficult for automated systems to achieve appropriate coverage of metaphors. Even when limited to a single target domain, detecting all metaphors would require knowledge of many metaphoric source domains to cover all relevant mappings (which themselves have to be known, too). As a result of this, many systems attempt to achieve high precision for specific mappings, rather than provide general coverage.

Many approaches (Gedigian et al., 2006; Krishnakumaran and Zhu, 2007; Mohler et al., 2013; Tsvetkov et al., 2013, and more) make use of manually crafted knowledge bases such as WordNet or FrameNet to establish concept domains. Other recent works establish domains via topic modeling (Shutova et al., 2010; Heintz et al., 2013), ad-hoc clustering (Strzalkowski et al., 2013) or by using semantic similarity vectors (Hovy et al., 2013).

We introduce term relevance as a measure for how *"out of place"* a word is in a given con-

Proceedings of the Second Workshop on Metaphor in NLP, pages 18–26,
Baltimore, MD, USA, 26 June 2014.

text. Our hypothesis is that words will often be out of place because they are not meant literally, but rather metaphorically. Term relevance is based on term frequency measures for target domains and mixed-domain data. The advantage of this approach is that it only requires knowledge of a text's literal target domain, but none about any source domains or conceptual mappings. As it does not require sentence structure information, it is also resistant to noisy data, allowing the use of large, uncurated corpora. While some works that utilize domain-mappings circumvent the need for pre-existing source data by generating it themselves (Strzalkowski et al., 2013; Mohler et al., 2013), our approach is truly source-independent.

We present a threshold classifier that uses term relevance as its only metric for metaphor detection. In addition we evaluate the impact of term relevance at different training sizes.

Our contributions are:

- We present a measure for non-literalness that only requires data for the literal domain(s) of a text.
- Our approach detects metaphors independently of their source domain.
- We report improvements for F_1 of 58% (stand-alone) and 68% (multi-feature) over a random baseline.

2 Term Relevance

We hypothesize that novel metaphoric language is marked by its unusualness in a given context. There will be a clash of domains, so the vocabulary will be noticeably different[1]. Therefore, an unusual choice of words may indicate metaphoricity (or non-literalness, at the least).

We measure this fact through a domain-specific *term relevance* metric. The metric consists of two features: *Domain relevance*, which measures whether a term is typical for the literal target domain of the text, and *common relevance*, which indicates terms that are so commonly used across domains that they have no discriminative power. If a term is not typical for a text's domain (i.e. has a low relevance), but is not very common either, it is considered a metaphor candidate. This can of course be extended to multiple literal domains (e.g. a political speech on fishing regulations will have both governance and maritime vocabulary), in which case a word is only considered as a metaphor if it is untypical for all domains involved.

2.1 Metric

We base *domain relevance* on TF-IDF (*term frequency inverse document frequency*), which is commonly used to measure the impact of a term on a particular document. Terms with a great impact receive high scores, while low scores are assigned to words that are either not frequent in the document or otherwise too frequent among other documents.

We adapt this method for *domain relevance (dr)* by treating all texts of a domain as a single "document". This new *term frequency inverse **domain** frequency* measures the impact of a term on the domain.

$$\mathrm{tf}_{dom}(t, d) = \frac{\#\text{ of term } t \text{ in domain } d}{\#\text{ of terms in domain } d} \quad (1)$$

$$\mathrm{idf}_{\mathrm{dom}}(t) = \log \frac{\#\text{ of domains}}{\#\text{ of domains containing } t} \quad (2)$$

$$\mathrm{dr}(t, d) = \mathrm{tf}_{\mathrm{dom}}(t, d) \times \mathrm{idf}_{\mathrm{dom}}(t) \quad (3)$$

To detect metaphors, we look for terms with low scores in this feature. However, due to the nature of TF-IDF, a low score might also indicate a word that is common among all domains. To filter out such candidates, we use normalized *document frequency* as a *common relevance* indicator.

$$\mathrm{cr}(t) = \frac{\#\text{ of documents containing } t}{\#\text{ of documents}} \quad (4)$$

In theory, we could also use *domain frequency* to determine common relevance, as we already compute it for domain relevance. However, as this reduces the feature's granularity and otherwise behaves the same (as long as domains are of equal size), we keep regular document frequency.

2.2 Generating Domains

We need an adequate number of documents for each domain of interest to compute *domain relevance* for it. We require specific data for the literal domain(s) of a text, but none for the metaphor's

[1]Strongly conventionalized metaphors will not meet this expectation, as they have become part of the target domain's vocabulary. Such metaphors can be easily detected by conventional means, such as knowledge bases. Our concern is therefore focused on novel metaphors.

source domains. This reduces the required number of domain data sets significantly without ruling out any particular metaphor mappings.

We extract domain-specific document collections from a larger general corpus, using the keyword query search of Apache Lucene[2], a software for indexed databases. The keywords of the query search are a set of seed terms that are considered typical literal terms for a domain. They can be manually chosen or extracted from sample data. For each domain we extract the 10,000 highest ranking documents and use them as the domain's dataset.

Afterwards, all remaining documents are randomly assigned to equally sized pseudo-domain datasets. These pseudo-domains allow us to compute the inverse of the *domain frequency* for the TF-IDF without the effort of assigning all documents to proper domains. The *document frequency* score that will be used as *common relevance* is directly computed on the documents of the complete corpus.

3 Data

We make use of two different corpora. The first is the domain-independent corpus required for computing term relevance. The second is an evaluation corpus for the *governance* domain on which we train and test our systems.

Both corpora are preprocessed using NLTK (Loper and Bird, 2002)[3]. After tokenization, stopwords and punctuation are removed, contractions expanded (e.g. *we've* to *we have*) and numbers generalized (e.g. *1990's* to *@'s*). The remaining words are reduced to their stem to avoid data sparsity due to morphological variation.

In case of the domain corpus, we also removed generic web document contents, such as HTML mark-up, JavaScript/CSS code blocks and similar boilerplate code[4].

3.1 Domain Corpus

As a basis for term relevance, we require a large corpus that is domain-independent and ideally also style-independent (i.e. not a newspaper corpus or Wikipedia). The world wide web meets these requirements. However, we cannot use public online search engines, such as Google or Bing, because they do not allow a complete overview of their indexed documents. As we require this provide to generate pseudo-domains and compute the inverse document/domain frequencies, we use a precompiled web corpus instead.

ClueWeb09[5] contains one billion web pages, half of which are English. For reasons of processing time and data storage, we limited our experiments to a single segment (`en0000`), containing 3 million documents. The time and storage considerations apply to the generation of term relevance values during preprocessing, due to the requirements of database indexing. They do not affect the actual metaphor detection process, therefore, we do not expect scalability to be an issue. As ClueWeb09 is an unfiltered web corpus, spam filtering was required. We removed 1.2 million spam documents using the *Waterloo Spam Ranking for ClueWeb09*[6] by Cormack et al. (2011).

3.2 Evaluation Corpus

Evaluation of the two classifiers is done with a corpus of documents related to the concept of *governance*. Texts were annotated for metaphoric phrases and phrases that are decidedly *in-domain*, as well as other factors (e.g. affect) that we will not concern ourselves with. The focus of annotation was to exhaustively mark metaphors, irrespective of their novelty, but avoid idioms and metonymy.

The corpus is created as part of the *MICS: Metaphor Interpretation in terms of Culturally-relevant Schemas* project by the U.S. Intelligence Advanced Research Projects Activity (IARPA). We use a snapshot containing 2,510 English sentences, taken from 312 documents. Of the 2,078 sentences that contain metaphors, 72% contain only a single metaphoric phrase. The corpus consists of around 48k tokens, 12% of which are parts of metaphors. Removing stopwords and punctuation reduces it to 23k tokens and slightly skews the distribution, resulting in 15% being metaphors.

We divide the evaluation data into 80% development and 20% test data. All reported results are based on test data. Where training data is required for model training (see section 5), ten-fold cross validation is performed on the development set.

[2] `http://lucene.apache.org/core/`

[3] `http://nltk.org`

[4] Mark-up and boilerplate removal scripts adapted from `http://love-python.blogspot.com/2011/04/html-to-text-in-python.html` and `http://effbot.org/zone/re-sub.htm`

[5] `http://lemurproject.org/clueweb09/`

[6] `http://plg.uwaterloo.ca/~gvcormac/clueweb09spam/`

Subdomain	Seed Terms
Executive	administer rule govern lead
Legislative	pass law regulate debate parliament
Judicial	judge hearing case rule case sentence
Administr.	administer manage issue permits analyze study facilitate obstruct
Enforcement	enforce allow permit require war make mandate defeat overcome
Economy	budget tax spend plan finances
Election	vote campaign canvass elect defeat form party create platform
Acceptance	government distrust (de)legitimize authority reject oppose strike flag protest pride salute march accept

Table 1: Manually selected seed terms for document search queries. The 10k documents with the highest relevance to the seeds are assigned to the subdomain cluster.

principl	financi	legisl	congress	crisi
corpor	famili	middl	compani	futur
countri	global	negoti	medicaid	unit
industri	promis	polici	constitut	save
obama	health	creat	capitalist	hous
clinton	nation	dream	american	busi
nuclear	amend	great	medicar	care
econom	million	feder	recoveri	job
commun	potenti	polit	freedom	law
prosper	energi	elect	program	new

Table 2: The fifty stems with the highest tf-idf score in the gold data. Used as seed terms for document search, generating a single *governance* domain. Stems are listed in no particular order.

4 Basic Classification

To gain an impression of the differentiating power of *tf-idf* in metaphor detection, we use a basic threshold classifier (tc) that uses domain relevance (dr) and common relevance (cr) as its only features. Given a word w, a target domain d and two thresholds δ and γ:

$$tc(w,d) = \begin{cases} \textbf{metaphor} & \text{if } dr(w,d) < \delta \\ & \text{and } cr(w) < \gamma \\ \textbf{literal} & \text{otherwise} \end{cases} \quad (5)$$

In cases where a text has more than one literal domain or multiple relevant subdomains are available, a word is only declared a metaphor if it is not considered literal for any of the (sub)domains.

4.1 Seed Terms

The threshold classifier is evaluated using two different sets of seed terms. The first set is composed of 60 manually chosen terms[7] from eight *governance* subdomains. These are shown in table 1. Each subdomain corpus consists of its 10,000 highest ranking documents. We do not subdivide the evaluation corpus into these subdomains. Rather, we assume that each sentence belongs to all eight subdomains[8], so a word is only considered a metaphor if it is non-literal for all of them. Preliminary experiments showed that this provides better performance than using a single domain corpus with more documents.

As the first set of seeds is chosen without statistical basis, the resulting clusters might miss important aspects of the domain. To ensure that our evaluation is not influenced by this, we also introduce a second seed set, which is directly based on the development data. As we mentioned in section 3.2, sentences in the MICS corpus were not only annotated for metaphoric phrases, but also for such that are decidedly domain-relevant. For example in the sentence *"Our **economy** is the **strongest** on earth"*, *economy* is annotated as in-domain and *strongest* as metaphor.

Based on these annotations, we divide the entire development data into three bags of words, one each for metaphor, in-domain and unmarked words. We then compute TF-IDF values for these bags, as we did for the domain clusters. The fifty terms[9] that score highest for the in-domain bag (i.e. those that make the texts identifiable as *governance* texts) are used as the second set of seeds (table 2). It should be noted that while the seeds were based on the evaluation corpus, the resulting term relevance features were nevertheless computed using clusters extracted from the web corpus.

[7]Terms were chosen according to human understanding of typical terms for *governance*. No optimization of the term choices was performed thereafter.

[8]As our evaluation corpus does not specify secondary domains for its texts (e.g. *fishery*), we chose not to define any further domains at this point.

[9]Various sizes were tried for the seed set. Using fifty terms offered the best performance, being neither too specific nor watering down the cluster quality. It is also close to the size of our first seed set.

	F_1	Prec	Rec
Random	0.222	0.142	0.500
All Metaphor	0.249	0.142	**1.000**
T-hold: Manual Seeds	**0.350**	**0.276**	0.478
T-hold: 50-best Seeds	0.346	0.245	***0.591***

Table 3: Summary of best performing settings for each threshold classifier model. Bold numbers indicate best performance; slanted bold numbers: best threshold classifier recall. All results are significantly different from the baselines with $p < 0.01$.

4.2 Evaluation

We evaluate and optimize our systems for the F_1 metric. In addition we provide precision and recall. Accuracy on the other hand proved an inappropriate metric, as the prevalence of literal words in our data resulted in a heavy bias. We evaluate on a token-basis, as half of the metaphoric phrases consist of a single word and less than 15% are more than three words long (including stopwords, which are filtered out later). Additionally, evaluating on a phrase-basis would have required grouping non-metaphor sections into phrases of a similar format.

Based on dev set performance, we choose a domain relevance threshold $\delta = 0.02$ and a common relevance threshold $\gamma = 0.1$. We provide a random baseline, as well as one that labels all words as metaphors, as they are the most frequently encountered baselines in related works. Results are shown in table 3.

Both seed sets achieve similar F-scores, beating the baselines by between 39% and 58%, but their precision and recall performance differs notably. Both models are significantly better than the baseline and significantly different from one another with $p < 0.01$. Significance was computed for a two-tailed t-test using `sigf` (Padó, 2006)[10].

Using manually chosen seed terms results in a recall rate that is slightly worse than chance, but it is made up by the highest precision. The fact that this was achieved without expert knowledge or term optimization is encouraging.

The classifier using the fifty best *governance* terms shows a stronger recall, most likely because the seeds are directly based on the development data, resulting in a domain cluster that more closely resembles the evaluation corpus. Precision, on the other hand, is slightly below that of the manual seed classifier. This might be an effect of the coarser granularity that a single domain score offers, as opposed to eight subdomain scores.

5 Multi-Feature Classification

Using term relevance as the only factor for metaphor detection is probably insufficient. Rather, we anticipate to use it either as a pre-filtering step or as a feature for a more complex metaphor detection system. To simulate the latter, we use an off-the-shelf machine learning classifier with which we test how *term relevance* interacts with other typical word features, such as *part of speech*. As we classify all words of a sentence, we treat the task as a binary sequential labeling task.

Preliminary tests were performed with HMM, CRF and SVM classifiers. CRF performance was the most promising. We use CRFsuite (Okazaki, 2007)[11], an implementation of conditional random fields that supports continuous values via scaling factors. Training is performed on the development set using ten-fold cross validation.

We present results for bigram models. Larger n-grams were inspected, too, including models with look-ahead functionality. While they were slightly more robust with regard to parameter changes, there was no improvement over the best bigram model. Also, as metaphor processing still is a low resource task for which sufficient training data is hard to come by, bigrams are the most accessible and representative option.

5.1 Training Features

We experimented with different representations for the term relevance features. As they are continuous values, they could be used as continuous features. Alternatively, they could be represented as binary features, using a cut-off value as for our threshold classifier. In the end, we chose a hybrid approach where thresholds are used to create binary features, but are also scaled according to their score. Thresholds were again determined on the dev set and set to $\delta = 0.02$ and $\gamma = 0.79$.

Each domain receives an individual domain relevance feature. There is only a single common rel-

[10] `http://www.nlpado.de/~sebastian/software/sigf.shtml`

[11] `http://www.chokkan.org/software/crfsuite/`

	F_1	Prec	Rec
All Metaphor	0.249	0.142	**1.000**
T-hold: Manual Seeds	0.350	0.276	0.478
CRF: Basic	0.187	0.706	0.108
CRF: Rel	0.219	0.683	0.130
CRF: PosLex	0.340	**0.654**	0.230
CRF: PosLexRel	**0.373**	0.640	***0.263***

Table 4: Summary of best performing settings for each CRF model. Bold numbers indicate best performance; slanted bold numbers: best CRF recall. All results are significantly different from the baseline with $p < 0.01$.

evance feature, as it is domain-independent. Surprisingly, we found no noteworthy difference in performance between the two seed sets (manual and 50-best). Therefore we only report results for the manual seeds.

In addition to term relevance, we also provide part of speech (pos) and lexicographer sense (lex) as generic features. The part of speech is automatically generated using NLTK's *Maximum Entropy POS Tagger*, which was trained on the *Penn Treebank*. To have a semantic feature to compare our relevance weights to, we include WordNet's lexicographer senses (Fellbaum, 1998), which are coarse-grained semantic classes. Where a word has more than one sense, the first was chosen. If no sense exists for a word, the word is given a `sense unknown` placeholder value.

5.2 Performance Evaluation

Performance of the CRF system (see table 4) seems slightly disappointing at first when compared to our threshold classifier. The best-performing CRF beats the threshold classifier by only two points of F-score, despite considerably richer training input. Precision and recall performance are reversed, i.e. the CRF provides a higher precision of 0.6, but only detects one out of four metaphor words. All models provide stable results for all folds, their standard deviation (about 0.01 for F_1) being almost equal to that of the baseline.

All results are significantly different from the baseline as well as from each other with $p < 0.01$, except for the precision scores of the three non-basic CRF models, which are significantly different from each other with $p < 0.05$.

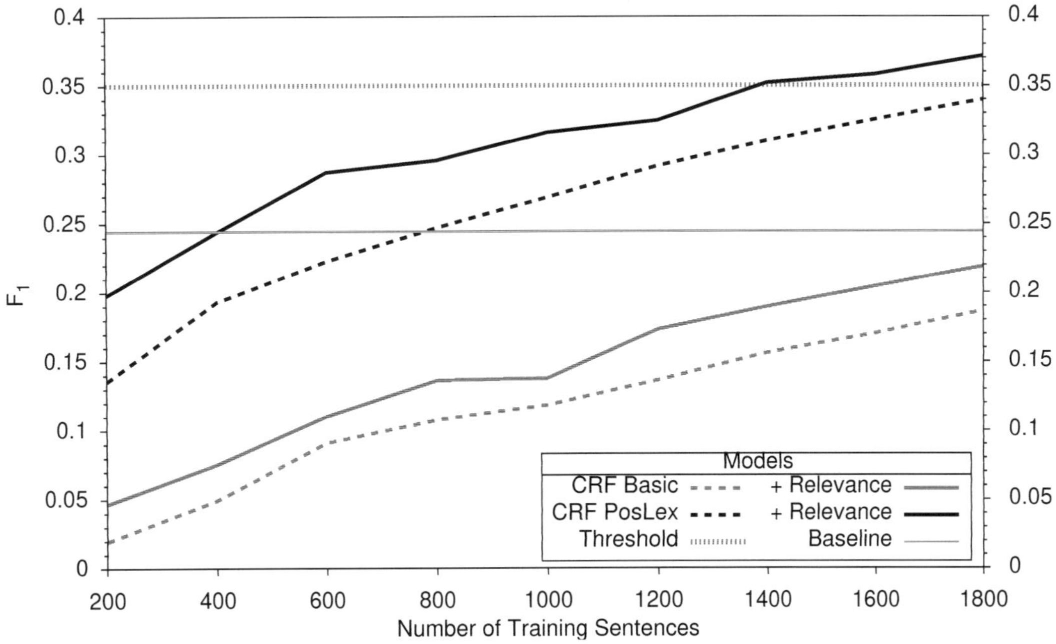

Figure 1: Performance curves for various training data sizes. Models with term relevance features (solid lines) outperform models without term relevance (dashed lines) at 1400 sentences. 1800 sentences represent the entire training set. Baseline (thin line) and best threshold classifier (dotted line) provided for reference.

Adding term relevance provides a consistent boost of 0.025 to the F-score. This boost, however, is rather marginal in comparison to the one provided by part of speech and lexicographer sense. A possible reason for this could be that the item weights learned during training correspond too closely to our term relevance scores, thus making them obsolete when enough training data is provided. The next section explores this possibility by comparing different amounts of training data.

5.3 Training Size Evaluation

With 2000 metaphoric sentences, the dataset we used was already among the largest annotated corpora. By reducing the amount of training data we evaluate whether term relevance is an efficient feature when data is sparse. To this end, we repeat our ten-fold cross validations, but withhold some of the folds from each training set.

Figure 1 compares the performance of CRF feature configurations with and without term relevance. In both cases adding term relevance outperforms the standard configuration's top performance with 400 sentences less, saving about a quarter of the training data.

In figure 2 we also visualize the relative gain that adding term relevance provides. As one can see, small datasets profit considerably more from our metric. Given only 200 sentences, the PosLex model receives 4.7 times the performance gain from term relevance it got at at maximum training size. The basic model has a factor of 6.8. This supports our assumption that term relevance is similar to the item weights learned during CRF training. As labeled training data is considerably more expensive to create than corpora for term relevance, this is an encouraging observation.

6 Related Work

For a comprehensive review on computational metaphor detection, see Shutova (2010). We limit our discussion to publications that were not covered by the review. While there are several papers evaluating on the same domain, direct comparison proved to be difficult, as many works were either evaluated on a sentence level (which our data was inappropriate for, as 80% of sentences contained metaphors) or did not provide coverage information. Another difference was that most evaluations were performed on balanced datasets, while our own data was naturally skewed for literal terms.

Strzalkowski et al. (2013) follow a related hypothesis, assuming that metaphors lack topical relatedness to in-domain words while being syntactically connected to them. Instead of using the metaphor candidate's relevance to a target domain corpus to judge relatedness, they circumvent the

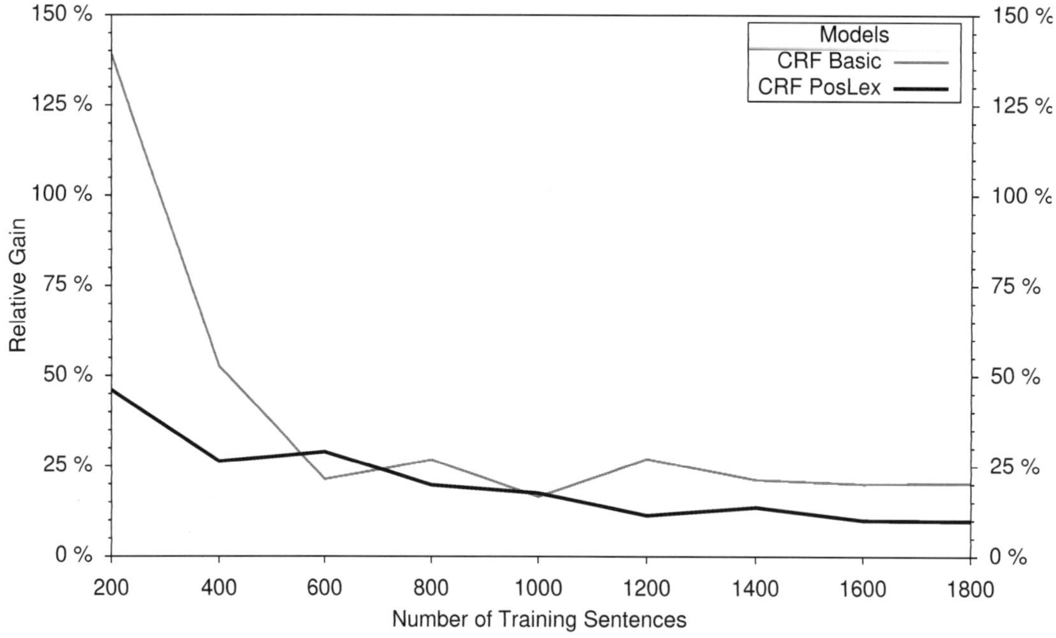

Figure 2: Relative performance gain of models obtained from addition of term relevance features.

need for pre-existing source data by generating ad-hoc collocation clusters and check whether the two highest ranked source clusters share vocabulary with the target domain. Further factors in their decision process are co-ocurrences in surrounding sentences and psycholinguistic imageability scores (i.e. how easy it is to form a mental picture of a word). Evaluating on data in the *governance* domain, they achieve an accuracy of 71% against an *all metaphor* baseline of 46%, but report no precision or recall.

Mohler et al. (2013) and Heintz et al. (2013) also evaluate on the *governance* domain. Rather than detecting metaphors at a word-level, both detect whether sentences contain metaphors. Mohler et al. (2013) compare semantic signatures of sentences to signatures of known metaphors. They, too, face a strong bias against the metaphor label and show how this can influence the balance between precision and recall. Heintz et al. (2013) classify sentences as containing metaphors if their content is related to both a target and source domain. They create clusters via topic modeling and, like us, use manually chosen seed terms to associate them with domains. Unlike our approach, theirs also requires seeds of all relevant source domains. They observe that identifying metaphors, even on a sentence level, is difficult even for experienced annotators, as evidenced by an inter-annotator agreement of $\kappa = 0.48$.

Shutova et al. (2010) use manually annotated seed sentences to generate source and target domain vocabularies via spectral clustering. The resulting domain clusters are used for selectional preference induction in verb-noun relations. They report a high precision of 0.79, but have no data on recall. Target concepts appearing in similar lexico-syntactic contexts are mapped to the same source concepts. The resulting mappings are then used to detect metaphors. This approach is notable for its combination of distributional clustering and selectional preference induction. Verbs and nouns are clustered into topics and linked through induction of selectional preferences, from which metaphoric mappings are deduced. Other works (Séaghdha, 2010; Ritter et al., 2010) use topic modeling to directly induce selectional preferences, but have not yet been applied to metaphor detection.

Hovy et al. (2013) generalize semantic preference violations from verb-noun relations to any syntactic relation and learn these in a supervised manner, using SVM and CRF models. The CRF is not the overall best-performing system, but achieves the highest precision of 0.74 against an all-metaphor baseline of 0.49. This is in line with our own observations. While they argue that metaphor detection should eventually be performed on every word, their evaluation is limited to a single expression per sentence.

Our work is also related to that of Sporleder and Li (2009) and Li and Sporleder (2010), in which they detect idioms through their lack of semantic cohesiveness with their context. Cohesiveness is measured via co-occurence of idiom candidates with other parts of a text in web searches. They do not make use of domains, basing their measure entirely on the lexical context instead.

7 Conclusion

We have presented term relevance as a non-literalness indicator and its use for metaphor detection. We showed that even on its own, term relevance clearly outperforms the baseline by 58% when detecting metaphors on a word basis.

We also evaluated the utility of term relevance as a feature in a larger system. Results for this were mixed, as the general performance of our system, a sequential CRF classifier, was lower than anticipated. However, tests on smaller training sets suggest that term relevance can help when data is sparse (as it often is for metaphor processing). Also, precision was considerably higher for CRF, so it might be more useful for cases where coverage is of secondary importance.

For future work we plan to reimplement the underlying idea of term relevance with different means. Domain datasets could be generated via topic modeling or other clustering means (Shutova et al., 2010; Heintz et al., 2013) and should also cover dynamically detected secondary target domains. Instead of using TF-IDF, term relevance can be modeled using semantic vector spaces (see Hovy et al. (2013)). While our preliminary tests showed better performance for CRF than for SVM, such a change in feature representation would also justify a re-evaluation of our classifier choice. To avoid false positives (and thus improve precision), we could generate ad-hoc source domains, like Strzalkowski et al. (2013) or Shutova et al. (2010) do, to detect overlooked literal connections between source and target domain.

Acknowledgements

We would like to thank the reviewers and proofreaders for their valuable input.

This research effort was in part supported by the German Academic Exchange Service (DAAD) scholarship program PROMOS with funds from the Federal Ministry of Education and Research (BMBF), awarded by the International Office of Saarland University as well as by the Intelligence Advanced Research Projects Activity (IARPA) via Department of Defense US Army Research Laboratory contract number W911NF-12-C-0025. The U.S. Government is authorized to reproduce and distribute reprints for Governmental purposes notwithstanding any copyright annotation thereon.

Disclaimer: The views and conclusions contained herein are those of the authors and should not be interpreted as necessarily representing the official policies or endorsements, either expressed or implied, of DAAD, BMBF, IARPA, DoD/ARL or the German or U.S. Government.

References

Gordon V. Cormack, Mark D. Smucker, and Charles L. A. Clarke. 2011. Efficient and effective spam filtering and re-ranking for large web datasets. *Information retrieval*, 14(5):441–465.

Christiane Fellbaum. 1998. ed. WordNet: an electronic lexical database. *MIT Press, Cambridge MA*, 1:998.

Matt Gedigian, John Bryant, Srini Narayanan, and Branimir Ciric. 2006. Catching metaphors. In *Proceedings of the HLT/NAACL-06 Workshop on Scalable Natural Language Understanding*, pages 41–48.

Ilana Heintz, Ryan Gabbard, Mahesh Srinivasan, David Barner, Donald S Black, Marjorie Freedman, and Ralph Weischedel. 2013. Automatic extraction of linguistic metaphor with lda topic modeling. *Proceedings of the ACL-13 Workshop on Metaphor*, page 58.

Dirk Hovy, Shashank Srivastava, Sujay Kumar Jauhar, Mrinmaya Sachan, Kartik Goyal, Huiying Li, Whitney Sanders, and Eduard Hovy. 2013. Identifying metaphorical word use with tree kernels. *Proceedings of the ACL-13 Workshop on Metaphor*, page 52.

Saisuresh Krishnakumaran and Xiaojin Zhu. 2007. Hunting elusive metaphors using lexical resources. In *Proceedings of the HLT/NAACL-07 Workshop on Computational Approaches to Figurative Language*, pages 13–20. Association for Computational Linguistics.

George Lakoff and Mark Johnson. 1980. *Metaphors we live by*, volume 111. University of Chicago Press.

Linlin Li and Caroline Sporleder. 2010. Using gaussian mixture models to detect figurative language in context. In *Proceedings of NAACL-10*, pages 297–300. Association for Computational Linguistics.

Edward Loper and Steven Bird. 2002. NLTK: The natural language toolkit. In *Proceedings of the COLING/ACL-02 workshop on Interactive presentation sessions*, pages 63–70. Association for Computational Linguistics.

Michael Mohler, David Bracewell, David Hinote, and Marc Tomlinson. 2013. Semantic signatures for example-based linguistic metaphor detection. *Proceedings of the ACL-13 Workshop on Metaphor*, page 27.

Naoaki Okazaki, 2007. *CRFsuite: a fast implementation of conditional random fields (CRFs).*

Sebastian Padó, 2006. *User's guide to `sigf`: Significance testing by approximate randomisation.*

Alan Ritter, Oren Etzioni, et al. 2010. A latent dirichlet allocation method for selectional preferences. In *ACT-10*, pages 424–434. Association for Computational Linguistics.

Diarmuid Ó Séaghdha. 2010. Latent variable models of selectional preference. In *Proceedings of ACL-10*, pages 435–444. Association for Computational Linguistics.

Ekaterina Shutova, Lin Sun, and Anna Korhonen. 2010. Metaphor identification using verb and noun clustering. In *Proceedings of COLING-10*, pages 1002–1010. Association for Computational Linguistics.

Ekaterina Shutova. 2010. Models of metaphor in NLP. In *Proceedings of ACL-10*, pages 688–697. Association for Computational Linguistics.

Caroline Sporleder and Linlin Li. 2009. Unsupervised recognition of literal and non-literal use of idiomatic expressions. In *Proceedings of EACL09*, pages 754–762. Association for Computational Linguistics.

Tomek Strzalkowski, George Aaron Broadwell, Sarah Taylor, Laurie Feldman, Boris Yamrom, Samira Shaikh, Ting Liu, Kit Cho, Umit Boz, Ignacio Cases, et al. 2013. Robust extraction of metaphors from novel data. *Proceedings of the ACL-13 Workshop on Metaphor*, page 67.

Yulia Tsvetkov, Elena Mukomel, and Anatole Gershman. 2013. Cross-lingual metaphor detection using common semantic features. *Proceedings of the ACL-13 Workshop on Metaphor*, page 45.

Yorick Wilks. 1978. Making preferences more active. *Artificial Intelligence*, 11(3):197–223.

Multi-dimensional abstractness in cross-domain mappings

Jonathan Dunn
Department of Computer Science / Illinois Institute of Technology
jonathan.edwin.dunn@gmail.com

Abstract

Metaphor is a cognitive process that shapes abstract target concepts by mapping them to concrete source concepts. Thus, many computational approaches to metaphor make reference, directly or indirectly, to the abstractness of words and concepts. The property of abstractness, however, remains theoretically and empirically unexplored. This paper implements a multi-dimensional definition of abstractness and tests the usefulness of each dimension for detecting cross-domain mappings.

1 Introduction

The idea of metaphor as cross-domain mapping goes back, at least, to Black (1954), who made explicit an earlier implicit view that linguistic metaphors depend upon non-linguistic (i.e., conceptual) connections between networks of concepts. Black's premises were later employed to represent groups of related linguistic metaphoric expressions using non-linguistic conceptual metaphors (for example, Reddy, 1979, and Lakoff & Johnson, 1980). Inherent in this approach to representing metaphor is the idea that metaphor is, at its core, a matter of cross-domain mapping (e.g., Lakoff, 1993); in other words, metaphor is a cognitive process that builds or maps connections between networks of concepts. The study of cognitive metaphor processes has largely focused on content-specific representations of such mappings within a number of content domains, such as TIME and IDEAS. Thus, a cross-domain mapping may be represented as something like ARGUMENT IS WAR.

Computational approaches to metaphor, however, have represented cross-domain mappings using higher-level properties like abstractness (Gandy, et al., 2013; Assaf, et al., 2013; Tsvetkov, et al., 2013; Turney, et al., 2011), semantic similarity (Li & Sporleder, 2010; Sporleder & Li, 2010), domain membership (Dunn, 2013a, 2013b), word clusters that represent semantic similarity (Shutova, et al. 2013; Shutova & Sun, 2013), and selectional preferences (Wilks, 1978; Mason, 2004). Most of these approaches rely on some concept of abstractness, whether directly (e.g., in terms of abstractness ratings) or indirectly (e.g., in terms of clusters containing abstract words). Further, these approaches have viewed abstractness as a one-dimensional scale between abstract and concrete concepts, with metaphor creating mappings from concrete source concepts to abstract target concepts.

Although both theoretical and computational treatments of metaphor depend upon the concept of abstractness, little has been done to either define or operationalize the notion. To fill this gap, this paper puts forward a multi-dimensional definition of abstractness and implements it in order to test the usefulness of the dimensions of abstractness for detecting cross-domain mappings.

2 Multi-dimensional abstractness

This approach recognizes four dimensions of abstractness: Domain of the Referent, Domain of the Sense, Fact-Status, and Function-Status, each of which has a range of values from more abstract to less abstract, as shown in Table 1. Domain refers to top-level categories in a hierarchical ontology as in, for example, ontological semantics (Nirenburg & Raskin, 2004), which uses four top-level domains: PHYSICAL, MENTAL, SOCIAL, ABSTRACT. Each concept belongs within a certain domain so that, at the highest level, cross-domain mappings can be represented as mappings between, for example, a PHYSICAL concept and an ABSTRACT concept. This dimension corresponds most with the traditional one-dimensional

Proceedings of the Second Workshop on Metaphor in NLP, pages 27–32,
Baltimore, MD, USA, 26 June 2014.

approach to abstractness.

Here we divide domain membership into two types: (i) Domain of the Sense and (ii) Domain of the Referent. The idea is that a concept may refer to an object in one domain but define properties of that concept relative to another domain. For example, the concept *teacher* refers to a PHYSICAL object, a human who has physical properties. At the same time, the concept *teacher* is defined or distinguished from other humans in terms of SOCIAL properties, such as being focused on the education of students. Thus, the referent of the concept is within the PHYSICAL domain but its sense is within the SOCIAL domain. This is also true, for example, of countries (e.g., Mexico) which refer to a PHYSICAL location but also to a SOCIAL entity, the government and people who reside in that physical location. It is important to distinguish sense and reference when searching for cross-domain mappings because many concepts inherently map between different domains in this way (and yet are not considered metaphoric). Within both types of Domain, ABSTRACT is the category with the highest abstractness and PHYSICAL with the least abstractness.

Fact-Status is an ontological property as opposed to a domain within a hierarchical ontology. It represents the metaphysical property of a concept's dependence on human consciousness (Searle, 1995). In other words, PHYSICAL-FACTS are those, like *rocks* and *trees*, which exist in the external world independent of human perceptions. NON-INTENTIONAL facts are involuntary human perceptions such as pain or fear. INTENTIONAL facts are voluntary products of individual human consciousness such as *ideas* and *opinions*. COLLECTIVE facts are products of the consciousness of groups of humans, such as *laws* and *governments*. Thus, all categories except for PHYSICAL-FACTS are dependent on human consciousness. NON-INTENTIONAL and INTENTIONAL facts depend only on individuals, and in this sense are less abstract than COLLECTIVE facts, which exist only if a group of humans agrees to recognize their existence. This dimension of abstractness measures how dependent on human consciousness and how socially-constructed a concept is, with COLLECTIVE facts being more socially-constructed (and thus more society-dependent) than the others.

The final dimension of abstractness is Function-Status, which reflects how embedded function information is in the sense of a concept. Function information is human-dependent, being present only as assumed by humans; thus, this dimension is also related to how human-centric a particular concept is. Many concepts have no function information embedded in them, for example *rock* or *tree*, and these are the least human-dependent. Some concepts have NON-AGENTIVE functions, sometimes called NATURAL functions; for example, the function of a *heart* is to pump blood. Some concepts have PHYSICAL-USE functions, in which the embedded function is a reflection of how humans use a physical object; for example, the function of a *hammer* is to drive nails. Finally, many concepts have embedded within them INSTITUTIONAL functions, those which perform a social function only insofar as a group of individuals agree that the social function is performed. For example, a group of individuals may declare that certain taxes will be collected on income; but if others do not consent to the performance of that function then it is not performed (e.g., if the group had no legal authority to do so). Thus, INSTITUTIONAL functions have the highest abstractness.

Property	**Value**
Domain of the Referent	Abstract Mental Social Physical
Domain of the Sense	Abstract Mental Social Physical
Fact-Status	Collective Intentional Non-Intentional Physical
Function	Institutional Physical-Use Non-Agentive None
Event-Status	Object State Process
Animacy	Human Animate Inanimate Undefined

Table 1: Concept properties and values.

In addition to these dimensions of abstractness, two properties are added in order to test how they interact with these dimensions of abstractness: Event-Status, distinguishing OBJECTS from STATES and PROCESSES, and Animacy, distinguishing HUMANS from ANIMATE non-humans and INANIMATE objects.

3 Implementation

The system has two main steps: first, the input text is mapped to concepts in the Suggested Upper Merged Ontology (Niles & Pease, 2001); second, features based on the ontological properties of these concepts are used to represent the input sentences as a feature vector. The text is processed using Apache OpenNLP for tokenization, named entity recognition, and part of speech tagging. Morpha (Minnen, et al., 2001) is used for lemmatization. At this point word sense disambiguation is performed using SenseRelate (Pedersen & Kolhatkar, 2009), mapping the lexical words to the corresponding WordNet senses. These WordNet senses are first mapped to SynSets and then to concepts in the SUMO ontology, using existing mappings (Niles & Pease, 2003). Thus, the input to the second part of the system is the set of SUMO concepts which are pointed to by the input text. The properties of these concepts are contained in a separate knowledge-base developed for this system and available from the author. Each concept in SUMO has a value for each of the concept properties. This value is fixed and is the same across all instances of that concept. Thus, SenseRelate disambiguates input text into WordNet synsets which are mapped onto SUMO concepts, at which point the mapping from concepts to concept properties is fixed.

Feature Type	Number
Relative value frequency	23
Main value / concepts	6
Other values / concepts	6
Number of value types	6
Total	41

Table 2: Concept properties and values.

The concept properties discussed above are used to create a total of 41 features as shown in Table 2: First, 23 features contain the total number of instances of each possible value for the properties in each sentence relative to the number of concepts present. Second, 6 features contain the relative frequency of the most common values of a property (the "main" value) and 6 features the relative frequency of all the other values (the "other" value). Third, 6 features contain the number of types of property values present in a sentence relative to the number of possible types.

4 Evaluation of the Features

We evaluated these features in a binary classification task using the VU Amsterdam Metaphor Corpus (Steen, et al., 2010), which consists of 200,000 words from the British National Corpus divided into four genres (academic, news, fiction, and spoken; the spoken genre was not evaluated) and annotated by five linguists. Metaphorically used prepositions have been untagged, as have ambiguously metaphoric sentences. Non-sentence fragments have been removed (e.g., titles and bylines), along with very short sentences (e.g., "He said.").

The first step was to evaluate the features individually for their usefulness in detecting metaphoric language, allowing us to ask theoretical questions about which dimensions of abstractness are most related to metaphor. The ClassifierSubSetEval feature in Weka (Hall, et al., 2009) was used with the logistic regression classifier on the full corpus with 10 fold cross-validation. Three different search algorithms were used to ensure that the best possible combination of variables was found: the Greedy Stepwise, Linear Forward Selection, and Rank Search algorithms. The final feature rating was computed by taking the reverse ranking given by the GreedyStepwise search (e.g., the top ranked feature out of 41 is given a 41) and adding the number of folds for which that feature was selected by the other two algorithms. Table 3 below shows the top variables, arranged by score.

An interesting finding from this selection process is that each of the concept properties made the list of the top 16 features in the form of the *Property: Other* feature. In other words, the number of minority values for each property is useful for detecting cross-domain mappings. Next, each of the values for the Function property was a top feature, while only two of the Domain-Sense and one of the Domain-Referent properties made the list. The properties of Animacy and Fact are represented by the number of types present in the utterance, and

Property	Feature	Score
Function	Other Values	45.5
Fact-Status	Other Values	41
Animacy	Types	39.1
Fact-Status	Collective	37.8
Event-Status	Other Values	31
Function	Non-Agentive	30.6
Animacy	Other Values	29.8
Function	Physical-Use	29.8
Fact-Status	Types	28.3
Domain-Sense	Abstract	27.1
Domain-Sense	Other Values	25.1
Domain-Sense	Mental	22.1
Domain-Referent	Social	21.8
Function	None	20.5
Function	Institutional	17.1
Domain-Referent	Other Values	12.8

Table 3: Top features.

Fact is also significant for the number of concepts with the Collective value. These are interesting, and unexpected, findings, because the most important properties for detecting metaphor are not the traditional Domain-defined notions of abstractness, either Sense or Referent, but rather those notions of abstractness which are tied to a concept's degree of dependence on human consciousness and degree of being socially-constructed.

Using these top 16 variables, a binary classification task was performed on the entire VU Amsterdam Corpus, prepared as described above, using the logistic regression algorithm with 10 fold cross-validation, giving the results shown below in Table 4. These results show that while the full set of 41 features performs slightly better than the select set of the top 16, the performance gain is fairly small. For example, the F-measure on the full corpus raises from 0.629, using only the top 16 variables, to 0.649 using the full set of 41 variables. Thus, a similar performance is achieved much more efficiently (at least, in terms of the evaluation of the feature vectors; the top 16 variables still require many of the other variables in order to be computed). More importantly, this shows that the different dimensions of abstractness can be used to detect cross-domain mappings, licensing the inference that each of these operationalizations of abstractness represents an important and independent property of cross-domain mappings.

Var.	Corpus	Prec.	Recall	F1
Select	Full	0.655	0.629	0.629
All	Full	0.672	0.691	0.649
Select	Academic	0.655	0.682	0.600
All	Academic	0.639	0.676	0.626
Select	Fiction	0.595	0.597	0.592
All	Fiction	0.642	0.642	0.642
Select	News	0.749	0.813	0.743
All	News	0.738	0.808	0.746

Table 4: Results of evaluation.

5 Relation between the dimensions of abstractness

In order to determine the relationship between these dimensions of abstractness, to be sure that they are not measuring only a single scale, principal components analysis was used to determine how many distinct groups are formed by the properties and their values. The written subset of the American and Canadian portions of the International Corpus of English, consisting of 44,189 sentences, was used for this task. The corpus was not annotated for metaphor; rather, the purpose is to find the relation between the features across both metaphor and non-metaphor, using the direct oblimin rotation method.

#	Main Features	CL.	Vari.
1	Domain-Sense: Types	.834	18.7%
	Domain-Ref.: Types	.816	
	Event-Status: Types	.808	
2	Fact-Status: Main	.778	14.2%
	Fact-Status: Physical	.774	
3	Domain-Sense: Physical	.509	11.1%
	Domain-Ref.: Physical	.548	
	Event-Status: Object	.451	
4	Fact-Status: Intentional	.990	10.6%
	Fact-Status: Collective	.990	
	Fact-Status: Other	.913	
5	Domain-Sense: Abstract	.997	6.6%
	Domain-Ref.: Abstract	.997	
6	Domain-Sense: Main	.851	5.8%
	Domain-Ref.: Main	.773	
7	Function: Physical-Use	.876	4.4%
8	Event-Status: Process	.574	3.6%
9	Animacy: Main	.800	2.9%
10	Function: Non-Agentive	.958	2.4%

Table 5: Grouped features.

This procedure identified 10 components with eigenvalues above 1 containing unique highest value features, accounting for a cumulative 83.2% of the variance. These components are shown in Table 5 along with the component loadings of the main features for each component and the amount of variance which the component explains. All features with component loadings within 0.100 of the top feature are shown.

These components show two important results: First, the division of the Domain property into Sense and Referent is not necessary because the two are always contained in the same components; in other words, these really constitute a single-dimension of abstractness. Second, Domain, Function, and Fact-Status are not contained in the same components, but rather remain distinguishable dimensions of abstractness.

The important point of this analysis of the relations between features is that, even for those systems which do not represent abstractness in this way (e.g., systems which use numeric scales instead of nominal attributes), the dimensions of abstractness used here do represent independent factors. In other words, there is more than one dimension of abstractness. Domain membership, which corresponds most closely to the traditional one-dimensional view, refers essentially to how concrete or physical a concept is. Thus, *love* is more abstract than *grass*, but no distinction is possible between *love* and *war*. Fact-Status refers to how dependent on human consciousness a concept is. PHYSICAL concepts do not depend upon humans in order to exist. Thus, PHYSICAL concepts will be represented with the same degree of abstractness by both the Domain and Fact-Status properties. However, Fact-Status adds distinctions between abstract concepts. For example, *ideas* are not physical, but *laws* are both non-physical and depend upon complex social agreements. Function-Status refers to how much of the definition of a concept is dependent upon Function information which is, ultimately, only present in human understandings of the concept. This dimension adds distinctions between even physical concepts. For example, *canes* are just as physical as *sticks*, but *cane* embeds function information, that the object is used to help a human to walk, and this function information is dependent upon human consciousness. These two additional and distinguishable dimensions of abstractness, then, operationalize how dependent a concept is on human consciousness and how socially-constructed it is.

Using the traditional one-dimensional approach to abstractness, not all metaphors have abstract target concepts. For example, in the metaphoric expressions "My car drinks gasoline" and "My surgeon is a butcher," the concepts CAR and SURGEON are both PHYSICAL concepts in terms of Domain, and thus not abstract. And yet these concepts are the targets of metaphors. However, the concept DRINKING, according to this system, has an INTENTIONAL Fact-Status, because it is an action which is performed purposefully, and thus is an action which only sentient beings can perform. It is more abstract, then, than a verb like *uses*, which would not be metaphoric. The second example, however, cannot be explained in this way, as both SURGEON and BUTCHER would have the same concept properties (they are not included in the knowledge-base; both map to HUMAN). This phrase occurs only twice in the 450+ million word Corpus of Contemporary American English, however, and represents a rare exception to the rule.

6 Conclusions

This paper has examined the notion of abstractness, an essential component of many theoretical and computational approaches to the cross-domain mappings which create metaphoric language. There are two important findings: First, of the four posited dimensions of abstractness, three were shown to be both (1) members of separate components and (2) useful for detecting metaphoric mappings. These three dimensions, Domain Membership, Fact-Status, and Function-Status, are different and distinguishable ways of defining and operationalizing the key notion of abstractness. Second, and perhaps more importantly, the Fact-Status and Function-Status dimensions of abstractness, which are not directly present in the traditional one-dimensional view of abstractness, were shown to be the most useful for detecting metaphoric mappings. Although more evidence is needed, this suggests that cross-domain mappings are mappings from less socially-constructed source concepts to more socially-constructed target concepts and from less consciousness-dependent source concepts to more consciousness-dependent target concepts. This multi-dimensional approach thus provides a more precise definition of abstractness.

References

Assaf, D., Neuman, Y., Cohen, Y., Argamon, S., Howard, N., Last, M., Koppel, M. 2013. Why "dark thoughts" aren't really dark: A novel algorithm for metaphor identification. *2013 IEEE Symposium on Computational Intelligence, Cognitive Algorithms, Mind, and Brain*: 60–65. Institute of Electrical and Electronics Engineers.

Black, M. 1954. Metaphor. *Proceedings of the Aristotelian Society, New Series*, 55: 273-294.

Dunn, J. 2013a. Evaluating the premises and results of four metaphor identification systems. *Proceedings of the 14th International Conference on Computational Linguistics and Intelligent Text Processing, Volume I*: 471-486. Berlin, Heidelberg: Springer-Verlag.

Dunn, J. 2013b. What metaphor identification systems can tell us about metaphor-in-language. *Proceedings of the First Workshop on Metaphor in NLP*: 1-10. Association for Computational Linguistics.

Gandy, L., Allan, N., Atallah, M., Frieder, O., Howard, N., Kanareykin, S., Argamon, S. 2013. Automatic Identification of Conceptual Metaphors With Limited Knowledge. *Proceedings of the 27th Conference on Artificial Intelligence*: 328–334. Association for the Advancement of Artificial Intelligence.

Hall, M., Frank, E., Holmes, G., Pfahringer, B., Reutemann, P., Witten, I. H. 2009. The WEKA data mining software. *ACM SIGKDD Explorations Newsletter*, 11(1): 10.

Lakoff, G. 1993. The contemporary theory of metaphor. *Metaphor and thought, 2nd edition*: 202-251. Cambridge, UK: Cambridge Univ Press.

Lakoff, G., Johnson, M. 1980. *Metaphors we live by*. Chicago: University Of Chicago Press.

Li, L., Sporleder, C. 2010a. Linguistic Cues for Distinguishing Literal and Non-literal Usages. *Proceedings of the 23rd International Conference on Computational Linguistics: Posters*: 683-691. Association for Computational Linguistics.

Li, L., Sporleder, C. 2010b. Using Gaussian Mixture Models to Detect Figurative Language in Context. *Human Language Technologies: The 2010 Annual Conference of the North American Chapter of the Association for Computational Linguistics*: 297–300. Association for Computational Linguistics.

Mason, Z. 2004. CorMet: A Computational, Corpus-Based Conventional Metaphor Extraction System. *Computational Linguistics*, 30(1), 23-44.

Minnen, G., Carroll, J., Pearce, D. 2001. Applied morphological processing of English. *Natural Language Engineering*, 7(3), 207-223.

Niles, I., Pease, A. 2001. Towards a standard upper ontology. *Proceedings of the International Conference on Formal Ontology in Information Systems*: 2-9. Association for Computing Machinery.

Niles, I., Pease, A. 2003. Linking lexicons and ontologies: Mapping WordNet to the Suggested Upper Merged Ontology. *Proceedings of the 2003 International Conference on Information and Knowledge Engineering*: 412-416. World Congress in Computer Science, Computer Engineering, and Applied Computing.

Nirenburg, S., Raskin, V. 2004. *Ontological Semantics*. Cambridge, MA: MIT Press.

Pedersen, T., Kolhatkar, V. 2009. WordNet::SenseRelate::AllWords–A broad coverage word sense tagger that maximimizes semantic relatedness. *Proceedings of Human Language Technologies: The 2009 Annual Conference of the North American Chapter of the Association for Computational Linguistics, Companion Volume: Demonstration Session*: 17-20. Association for Computational Linguistics.

Reddy, M. 1979. The conduit metaphor: A case of frame conflict in our language about language. *Metaphor and Thought, 1st edition*: 284-310. Cambridge, UK: Cambridge Univ Press.

Searle, J. 1995. *The construction of social reality*. New York: The Free Press.

Shutova, E., Sun, L. 2013. Unsupervised Metaphor Identification using Hierarchical Graph Factorization Clustering. *Proceedings of Human Language Technologies: The 2013 Annual Conference of the North American Chapter of the Association for Computational Linguistics*: 978-988. Association for Computational Linguistics.

Shutova, E., Teufel, S., Korhonen, A. 2013. Statistical Metaphor Processing. *Computational Linguistics*, 39(2), 301-353.

Steen, G. J., Dorst, A. G., Herrmann, J. B., Kaal, A. A., Krennmayr, T. 2010. Metaphor in usage. *Cognitive Linguistics*, 21(4), 765-796.

Tsvetkov, Y., Mukomel, E., Gershman, A. 2013. Cross-Lingual Metaphor Detection Using Common Semantic Features. *Proceedings of the First Workshop on Metaphor in NLP*: 45-51. Association for Computational Linguistics.

Turney, P. D., Neuman, Y., Assaf, D., Cohen, Y. 2011. Literal and Metaphorical Sense Identification Through Concrete and Abstract Context. *Proceedings of the Conference on Empirical Methods in Natural Language Processing*: 680-690. Association for Computational Linguistics.

Wilks, Y. 1978. Making preferences more active. *Artificial Intelligence*, 11(3), 197-223.

Abductive Inference for Interpretation of Metaphors

Ekaterina Ovchinnikova*, Ross Israel*, Suzanne Wertheim+,

Vladimir Zaytsev*, Niloofar Montazeri*, Jerry Hobbs*

* USC ISI, 4676 Admiralty Way, CA 90292, USA
{katya,israel,vzaytsev,niloofar,hobbs}@isi.edu
+ Worthwhile Research & Consulting, 430 1/2 N Genesee Av., Los Angeles, CA 90036, USA
worthwhileresearch@gmail.com

Abstract

This paper presents a metaphor interpretation pipeline based on abductive inference. In this framework following (Hobbs, 1992) metaphor interpretation is modelled as a part of the general discourse processing problem, such that the overall discourse coherence is supported. We present an experimental evaluation of the proposed approach using linguistic data in English and Russian.

1 Introduction

In this paper, we elaborate on a semantic processing framework based on a mode of inference called *abduction*, or inference to the best explanation. In logic, abduction is a kind of inference which arrives at an explanatory hypothesis given an observation. (Hobbs et al., 1993) describe how abduction can be applied to the discourse processing problem, viewing the process of interpreting sentences in discourse as the process of providing the best explanation of why the sentence would be true. (Hobbs et al., 1993) show that abductive reasoning as a discourse processing technique helps to solve many pragmatic problems such as reference resolution, the interpretation of noun compounds, detection of discourse relations, etc. as a by-product. (Hobbs, 1992) explains how abduction can be applied to interpretation of metaphors.

The term *conceptual metaphor* (CM) refers to the understanding of one concept or conceptual domain in terms of the properties of another (Lakoff and Johnson, 1980; Lakoff, 1987). For example, development can be understood as movement (e.g., *the economy moves forward, the engine of the economy*). In other words, a conceptual metaphor consists in mapping a *target* conceptual domain (e.g., economy) to a *source* domain (e.g., vehicle) by comparing their properties (e.g., an economy develops like a vehicle moves). In text, conceptual metaphors are represented by *linguistic metaphors* (LMs), i.e. natural language phrases expressing the implied comparison of two domains.

We present a metaphor interpretation approach based on abduction. We developed an end-to-end metaphor interpretation system that takes text potentially containing linguistic metaphors as input, detects linguistic metaphors, maps them to conceptual metaphors, and interprets conceptual metaphors in terms of both logical predicates and natural language expressions. Currently, the system can process linguistic metaphors mapping predefined target and source domains.

We perform an experimental evaluation of the proposed approach using linguistic data in two languages: English and Russian. We select target concepts and generate potential sources for them as described at *github.com/MetaphorExtractionTools/mokujin*. For top-ranked sources, we automatically find corresponding linguistic metaphors. These linguistic metaphors are each then validated by three expert linguists. For the validated linguistic metaphors, we generate natural language interpretations, which are also validated by three experts.

2 Related Work

Automatic interpretation of linguistic metaphors is performed using two principal approaches: 1) deriving literal paraphrases for metaphorical expressions from corpora (Shutova, 2010; Shutova et al., 2012) and 2) reasoning with manually coded knowledge (Hobbs, 1992; Narayanan, 1999; Barnden and Lee, 2002; Agerri et al., 2007; Veale and Hao, 2008).

(Shutova, 2010; Shutova et al., 2012) present methods for deriving paraphrases for linguistic metaphors from corpora. For example, the metaphorical expression "a carelessly *leaked* re-

Proceedings of the Second Workshop on Metaphor in NLP, pages 33–41,
Baltimore, MD, USA, 26 June 2014.

port" is paraphrased as "a carelessly *disclosed* report". This approach currently focuses on single-word metaphors expressed by verbs only and does not explain the target–source mapping.

The KARMA (Narayanan, 1999) and the ATT-Meta (Barnden and Lee, 2002; Agerri et al., 2007) systems perform reasoning with manually coded world knowledge and operate mainly in the source domain. The ATT-Meta system takes logical expressions that are representations of a small discourse fragment as input; i.e., it does not work with natural language. KARMA focuses on dynamics and motion in space. For example, the metaphorical expression *the government is stumbling in its efforts* is interpreted in terms of motion in space: stumbling leads to falling, while falling is a conventional metaphor for failing.

(Veale and Hao, 2008) suggest to derive common-sense knowledge from WordNet and corpora in order to obtain concept properties that can be used for metaphor interpretation. Simple inference operations, i.e. insertions, deletions and substitution, allow the system to establish links between target and source concepts.

(Hobbs, 1992) understands metaphor interpretation as a part of the general discourse processing problem. According to Hobbs, a metaphorical expression should be interpreted in context. For example, *John is an elephant* can be best interpreted as "John is clumsy" in the context *Mary is graceful, but John is an elephant.* In order to obtain context-dependent interpretations, (Hobbs, 1992) uses abductive inference linking parts of the discourse and ensuring discourse coherence.

3 Metaphor Interpretation System

Our abduction-based metaphor interpretation system is shown in Fig. 1. Text fragments possibly containing linguistic metaphors are given as input to the pipeline. The text fragments are parsed and converted into logical forms (section 3.1). The logical forms are input to the abductive reasoner (section 3.2) that is informed by a knowledge base (section 4). The processing component labelled "CM extractor & scorer" extracts conceptual metaphors from the logical abductive interpretations and outputs scored CMs and Target-Source mappings (section 3.3). The Target-Source mappings are then translated into natural language expressions by the NL generator module (section 3.4).

3.1 Logical Form Generation

A *logical form* (LF) is a conjunction of propositions which have argument links showing relationships among phrase constituents. We use logical representations of natural language texts as described in (Hobbs, 1985). In order to obtain LFs we convert dependency parses into logical representations in two steps: 1) assign arguments to each lemma, 2) apply rules to dependencies in order to link arguments.

Consider the dependency structure for the sentence, *John decided to leave*: `[PRED decide [SUBJ John] [OBJ leave]]`. First, we generate unlinked predicates for this structure: $John(e_1, x_1) \wedge decide(e_2, x_2, x_3) \wedge leave(e_3, x_4)$. Then, based on the dependency labels, we link argument x_1 with x_2, x_3 with e_3, and x_1 with x_4 to obtain the following LF: $John(e_1, x_1) \wedge decide(e_2, x_1, e_3) \wedge leave(e_3, x_1)$.

LFs are preferable to dependency structures in this case because they generalize over syntax and link arguments using long-distance dependencies. Furthermore, we need logical representations in order to apply abductive inference.

In order to produce logical forms for English, we use the *Boxer* semantic parser (Bos et al., 2004). As one of the possible formats, *Boxer* outputs logical forms of sentences in the style of (Hobbs, 1985). For Russian, we use the *Malt* dependency parser (Nivre et al., 2006). We developed a converter turning Malt dependencies into logical forms in the style of (Hobbs, 1985).[1]

3.2 Abductive Inference

In order to detect conceptual metaphors and infer explicit mappings between target and source domains, we employ a mode of inference called weighted abduction (Hobbs et al., 1993). This framework is appealing because it is a realization of the observation that we understand new material by linking it with what we already know.

Abduction is inference to the best explanation. Formally, logical abduction is defined as follows:

Given: Background knowledge B, observations O, where both B and O are sets of first-order logical formulas,
Find: A hypothesis H such that $H \cup B \models O$, $H \cup B \not\models \perp$, where H is a set of first-order logical formulas.

[1]The converter is freely available at *https://github.com/eovchinn/Metaphor-ADP*.

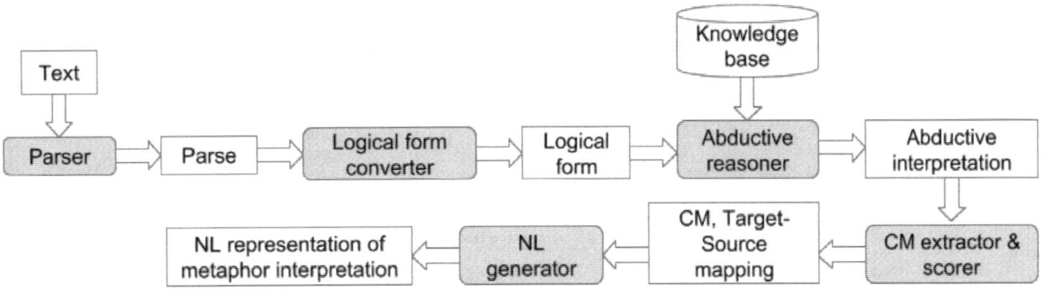

Figure 1: Abduction-based metaphor interpretation system.

Typically, there exist several hypotheses H explaining O. To rank hypotheses according to plausibility and select the best hypothesis, we use the framework of weighted abduction (Hobbs et al., 1993). Frequently, the best interpretation results from identifying two entities with each other, so that their common properties only need to be proved or assumed once. Weighted abduction favors those interpretations that link parts of observations together and supports discourse coherence, which is crucial for discourse interpretation.

According to (Hobbs, 1985), metaphor interpretation can be modelled as abductive inference revealing conceptual overlap between the target and the source domain. Consider the abductive interpretation produced for the sentence *We intend to cure poverty*, Fig. 2. In the top line of the figure, we have the LF (cf. Sec. 3.1), where we can see that a *person* (x_1) is the agent for the verbs *intend* (e_1) and *cure* (e_2) and that *poverty* (x_2) is the object of *cure*. In the first box in the next row, we see that *cure* invokes the source concepts of DISEASE, CURE, and DOCTOR, where DISEASE is the object of CURE, and DOCTOR is the subject. In the same row, we see that *poverty* invokes the POVERTY concept in the target domain. Importantly, POVERTY and DISEASE share the same argument (x_2), which refers to *poverty*.

The next row contains two boxes with ellipses, representing long chains of common-sense inferences in the source and target domains of DISEASE and POVERTY, respectively. For DISEASE we know that linguistic tokens such as *illness, sick, disease*, etc. cause the afflicted to experience loss of health, loss of energy, and a general lack of productivity. For POVERTY, we know that tokens such as *poor, broke, poverty* mean that the experiencer of poverty lacks money to buy things, take care of basic needs, or have access to transportation. The end result of both of these frameworks is that the affected individuals (or communities) cannot function at a normal level, with respect to unaffected peers. We can use this common meaning of causing the individual to not function to link the target to the source.

The next three rows provide the mapping from the meaning of the source (CURE, DOCTOR, DISEASE) concepts to the target concept (POVERTY). As explained above, we can consider DISEASE as a CAUSING-AGENT that can CAUSE NOT FUNCTION; POVERTY can be explained the same way, at a certain level of abstraction. Essentially, the interpretation of *poverty* in this sentence is that it causes some entity not to function, which is what a DISEASE does as well. For CURE, we see that *cure* can CAUSE NOT EXIST, while looking for a CAUSING-AGENT (*person*) and an EXISTING DISEASE (*poverty*).

In our system, we use the implementation of weighted abduction based on Integer Linear Programming (ILP) (Inoue and Inui, 2012), which makes the inference scalable.

3.3 CM Extractor and Scorer

The abductive reasoning system produces an interpretation that contains mappings of lexical items into Target and Source domains. Any Target-Source pair detected in a text fragment constitutes a potential CM. For some text fragments, the system identifies multiple CMs. We score Target-Source pairs according to the length of the dependency path linking them in the predicate-argument structure. Consider the following text fragment:

opponents argue that any state attempting to force an out-of-state business to do its dirty work of tax collection violates another state's right to regulate its own corporate residents and their commerce

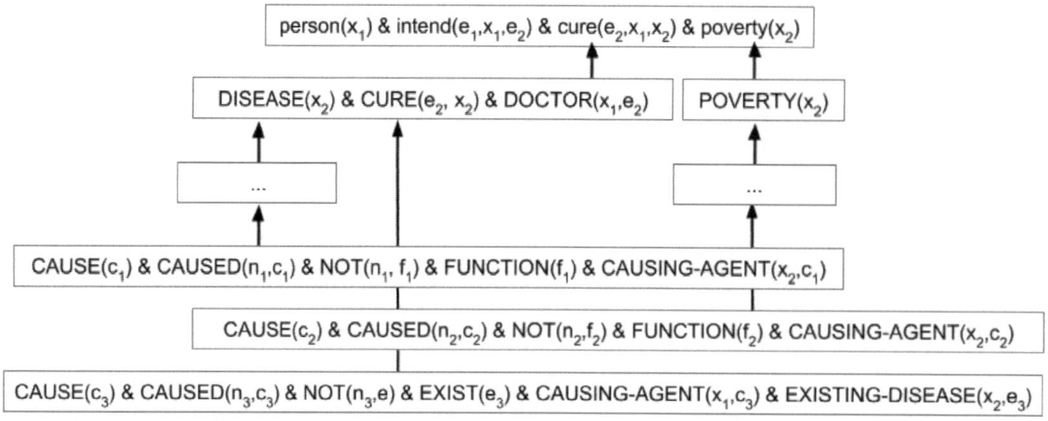

Figure 2: Abductive interpretation for the sentence *We intend to cure poverty.*

Suppose our target domain is TAXATION, triggered by *tax collection* in the sentence above. In our corpus, we find realizations of the CM TAXATION is an ENEMY (*fight against taxes*). The lexeme *opponent* triggers the STRUGGLE/ENEMY domain. However, the sentence does not trigger the CM TAXATION is an ENEMY. Instead, it instantiates the CM TAXATION is DIRT (*dirty work of tax collection*). The length of the dependency path between *dirty* and *tax* is equal to 2, whereas the path between *opponent* and *tax* is equal to 9. Therefore, our procedure ranks TAXATION is DIRT higher, which corresponds to the intuition that target and source words should constitute a syntactic phrase in order to trigger a CM.

3.4 NL Representation of Metaphor Interpretation

The output of the abduction engine is similar to the logical forms provided in Fig. 2. In order to make the output more reader friendly, we produce a natural language representation of the metaphor interpretation using templates for each CM. For example, the text *their rivers of money mean they can offer far more than a single vote* would invoke the WEALTH is WATER CM, and the abduction engine would output: LARGE-AMOUNT[river], THING-LARGE-AMOUNT[money]. We then take this information and use it as input for the NL generation module to produce: *"river" implies that there is a large amount of "money".*

4 Knowledge Base

In order to process metaphors with abduction, we need a knowledge base that encodes the information about the source domain, the target domain, and the relationships between sources and targets. We develop two distinct sets of axioms: lexical axioms that encode lexical items triggering domains, and mapping axioms that encode knowledge used to link source and target domains. We will discuss the details of each axiom type next.

4.1 Lexical Axioms

Every content word or phrase that can be expected to trigger a source or target domain is included as a lexical axiom in the knowledge base. For example, the STRUGGLE domain contains words like *war, fight, combat, conquer, weapon,* etc. An example of how a lexical axiom encodes the system logic is given in (1). On the left side, we have the linguistic token, *fight*, along with its part-of-speech, *vb*, and the argument structure for verbs where e_0 is the eventuality (see (Hobbs, 1985)) of the action of fighting, x is the subject of the verb, and y is the object. On the right side, STRUGGLE is linked to the action of fighting, the subject is marked as the AGENT, and the object is marked as the ENEMY.

(1) $\textit{fight-vb}(e_0, x, y) \rightarrow STRUGGLE(e_0) \wedge AGENT(x, e_0) \wedge ENEMY(y, e_0)$

The lexicon is not limited to single-token entries; phrases can be included as single entries; For example, the ABYSS domain has phrases such as *climb out of* as a single entry. Encoding phrases often proves useful, as function words can often help to distinguish one domain from others. In this case, climbing *out of* something usually denotes an abyss, whereas climbing *up* or *on* usually does not. The lexical axioms also include the POS for each word. Thus a word like *fight* can be entered as both a noun and a verb. In cases where a single lexical axiom could be applied to multiple domains, one can create multiple entries for the axiom with different domains and assign weights so that a certain domain is preferred over others.

Initial lexical axioms for each domain were developed based on intuition about each domain. We then utilize ConceptNet (Havasi et al., 2007) as a source for semi-automatically extracting a large-scale lexicon. ConceptNet is a multilingual semantic network that establishes links between words and phrases. We query ConceptNet for our initial lexical axioms to return a list of related words and expressions.

4.2 Mapping Axioms

Mapping axioms provide the underlying meanings for metaphors and link source and target domains. All of these axioms are written by hand based on common-sense world knowledge about each target-source pair. For each CM, we consider a set of LMs that are realizations of this CM in an effort to capture inferences that are common for all of the LMs. We consider the linguistic contexts of the LMs and overlapping properties of the target and source domains derived from corpora as described in section 5.1.

We will outline the process of axiomatizing the STRUGGLE domain here. We know that a verb like *fight* includes concepts for the struggle itself, an agent, and an enemy. In the context of a STRUGGLE, an enemy can be viewed as some entity a that attempts to, or actually does, inhibit the functioning of some entity b, often through actual physical means, but also psychologically, economically, etc. The struggle, or fight, itself then, is an attempt by a to rid itself of b so that a can ensure normal functionality. So, given a phrase like *poverty is our enemy*, the intended meaning is that poverty is hindering the functionality of some entity (an individual, a community, a country, etc.) and is seen as a problem that must be fought, i.e. eliminated. In a phrase like *the war against poverty*, war refers to an effort to stop the existence of poverty. These inferences are supported by the overlapping property propositions extracted from English Gigaword as described in Sec. 5.1, e.g., *scourge of X, country fights X, country pulls of X, suffer from X, fight against X.*

To extend the example in (1), consider (2). Here, we encode a STRUGGLE action, e.g. *fight*, as CAUSE NOT EXIST, the AGENT of the fight as CAUSING-AGENT, and the ENEMY as EXISTING-THING. Then, for a verb phrase like *we fight poverty*, *we* is the AGENT that engages in causing *poverty*, the ENEMY, to not exist.

(2) $STRUGGLE(e_0) \wedge AGENT(x, e_0) \wedge ENEMY(y, 2_0) \rightarrow CAUSE(e_0) \wedge CAUSED(n, e_0) \wedge NOT(n, ex) \wedge EXIST(ex) \wedge CAUSING-AGENT(x, e_0) \wedge EXISTING-THING(y, ex)$

We use 75 mapping axioms to cover the valid LMs discussed in Sec. 5.2. Some interesting trends emerge when examining the core meanings of the LMs. Following (Hobbs, 2005), we found that over 65% of the valid LMs in this study could be explained in terms of causality. The next most prevalent aspect that these metaphors touch upon is that of functionality (nearly 35%), with some of these overlapping with the causality aspect where the meaning has to do with *X causing Y* to *function* or *not function*.

Many of the CMs covered in this study have fairly transparent interpretations based on these ideas of causality and functionality, such as POVERTY is DISEASE, where the main underlying meaning is that a disease causes the sufferer not to function properly. However, for some CMs, the interpretation can be more difficult to pin down. For example, the interpretation of WEALTH is a GAME is quite opaque. Given a sentence such as, *Wealth is a game and you better start playing the game*, there are no obvious connections to concepts such as causality or functionality. Instead, *game* raises such ideas as competition, winning, and losing. In the literal context of a game, the competition itself, who the competitors are, and what it means to win or lose are usually clearly defined, but this is not so when speaking metaphorically about wealth. To derive a meaning of *game* that can apply to wealth, we must look at a higher level of abstraction and define *game* as the instantiation of a positive or negative outcome, i.e. to *win* is to achieve a positive outcome, or gain *wealth*. In the same sentence *play* implies that some voluntary action must be taken to achieve a positive outcome.

For some metaphors, a simple transfer of the source properties to the target does not result in a coherent interpretation at all. Given, for example, the CM POVERTY is a PRICE, one LM from this study is, *poverty is the price of peace*. In this case, the meaning has to do with some notion of an exchange, where a negative consequence must be accepted in order to achieve a desired outcome. However, the metaphorical meaning of *price* differs from the literal meaning of the word. In literal contexts, *price* refers to an amount of money or goods with inherent value that must be given to acquire something; the buyer has a supply of money or goods that they willingly exchange for their desired item. In the metaphorical sense, though, there often is no buyer, and there is certainly not an inherent value that can be assigned to *poverty*, nor can one use a supply of it to acquire *peace*.

Another issue concerns cultural differences. While writing the axioms to deal with English and Russian source-target pairs we noticed that a majority of the axioms applied equally well to both languages. However, there are some subtle differences of aspect that impact the interpretation of similar CMs across the two languages. Looking again at the WEALTH is a GAME metaphor, the Russian interpretation involves some nuance of a lack of importance about the subject that does not seem to be present in English when using words like *game* and *play*. Note that there may be some notion of carelessness for English (see Sec. 5.3), but for Russian, the notion of being carefree, which is not the same as careless, about wealth has a strong prevalence.

5 Experimental Validation

5.1 Source Generation

Following from the definition of metaphor, the target and the source domain share certain properties. In natural language, concepts and properties are represented by words and phrases. There is a long-standing tradition for considering computational models derived from word co-occurrence statistics as being capable of producing reasonable property-based descriptions of concepts (Baroni and Lenci, 2008). We use proposition stores to derive salient properties of concepts that can be potentially compared in a metaphor.

A *proposition store* is a collection of propositions such that each proposition is assigned its frequency in a corpus. Propositions are tuples of words that have a determined pattern of syntactic relations among them (Clark and Harrison, 2009; Peñas and Hovy, 2010; Tsao and Wible, 2013). For example, the following propositions can be extracted from the sentence *John decided to go to school*:

(*NV John decide*)
(*NV John go*)
(*NVPN John go to school*)
...

We generated proposition stores from parsed English Gigaword (Parker et al., 2011) and Russian ruWac (Sharoff and Nivre, 2011). Given the proposition stores, we generate potential sources for a seed target lexeme l in three steps:

1. Find all propositions P_l containing l.
2. Find all potential source lexemes S such that for each $s \in S$ there are propositions p, p' in the proposition store such that l occurs at position i in p and s occurs at position i in p'. The set of propositions containing l and s at the same positions is denoted by $P_{l,s}$.
3. Weight potential sources $s \in S$ using the following equation:

$$weight_l(s) = \sum_{p \in P_{l,s}} weight_l(t), \qquad (1)$$

The source generation procedure and its validations are described in detail at *github.com/MetaphorExtractionTools/mokujin*.[2] In the experiment described below, we generated potential sources for the target domains of POVERTY and WEALTH.

5.2 Linguistic Metaphors Extraction and Validation

For each potential CM, we look for supporting LMs in corpora. A a large number of LMs supporting a particular CM suggests that this CM might be cognitively plausible. We use a simple method for finding LMs. If a target lexeme and a source lexeme are connected by a dependency relation in a sentence, then we assume that this dependency structure contains a LM. For example, in the phrases *medicine against poverty* and *chronic poverty*, the target word (*poverty*) is related via dependency arc with the source words (*medicine, chronic*). LMs were extracted from English Gigaword (Parker et al., 2011) and Russian ruWac (Sharoff and Nivre, 2011).

For the generated CMs, we select seed lexemes for target and source domains. We expand the

[2]The tools for generating proposition stores and the obtained resources are freely available at *https://ovchinnikova.me/proj/metaphor.html*.

sets of these target and source lexemes with semantically related lexemes using English and Russian ConceptNet (Speer and Havasi, 2013) and top ranked patterns from the proposition stores. For example, the expansion of the lexeme *disease* results in the following set of lexemes: {*disease, symptom, syndrome, illness, unwellness, sickness, sick, medicine, treatment, treat, cure, doctor, ...* }

For each language, we select 20 top-ranked sources per target. Then we randomly select at most 10 sentences per each target-source pair. These sentences are validated by 3 linguist experts each. For each sentence, the experts are asked if it contains a metaphor comparing an indicated target domain with an indicated source domain. The inter-annotator agreement on the validation task is defined as the percentage of judgements on which the three experts agree. Agreement is 81% for English and 80% for Russian.

Tables 1 and 2 show 10 potential sources per target with the best agreement. Column ALL provides the number of sentences per a proposed CM such that all experts agreed that the sentence contains a metaphor. Column TWO provides the number of sentences such that any two experts agreed on, and Column ONE shows the number of sentences such that a single expert thought it contained a metaphor.

target	source	ALL	TWO	ONE
wealth	blood	10	10	10
	water	9	10	10
	drug	9	10	10
	food	9	9	10
	body	9	9	10
	power	8	9	10
	game	8	9	9
	security	7	9	10
	resource	7	7	9
	disease	7	8	9
poverty	war	10	10	10
	abyss	10	10	10
	violence	9	9	10
	price	8	9	9
	location	7	8	8
	disease	7	7	7
	crime	4	5	6
	crop	3	7	9
	terrorism	3	3	5
	cost	2	3	7

Table 1: Validation of English linguistic metaphors found for potential sources.

5.3 Metaphor Interpretation Validation

Metaphor interpretations were generated for positively validated linguistic metaphors, as described

богатство (wealth)	энергия (energy)	10	10	10
	вода (water)	10	10	10
	свобода (freedom)	10	10	10
	власть (power)	9	10	10
	бог (god)	9	10	10
	кровь (blood)	9	10	10
	путь (way)	9	10	10
	игра (game)	8	10	10
	слава (glory)	4	5	5
	товар (ware)	3	8	10
бедность (poverty)	пропасть (abyss)	10	10	10
	враг (enemy)	9	10	10
	болезнь (disease)	9	9	9
	власть (power)	8	10	10
	тело (body)	6	6	6
	боль (pain)	5	10	10
	отчаяние (despair)	5	10	10
	цена (price)	4	4	4
	смерть (death)	3	5	6
	страх (fear)	3	9	10

Table 2: Validation of Russian linguistic metaphors found for potential sources.

in Sec. 3.4. Each interpretation was validated by three expert linguists. We calculated strict and relaxed agreement for the validated data. Strict agreement is calculated over three categories: correct (C), partially correct (P), and incorrect (I). Relaxed agreement is calculated over two categories: C/P and I. Partially correct means that the validator felt that something was missing from the interpretation, but that what was there was not wrong. Table 3 presents the validation results for both languages. As can be seen in the table, strict agreement (AgrS) is 62% and 52% and strict system accuracy (AccS ALL) is 62% and 50% for English and Russian, respectively. Relaxed agreement (AgrR) results is 93% and 83%, and relaxed accuracy (AccR ALL) is 91% and 78%.

Validators often marked things as only partially correct if they felt that the interpretation was lacking some aspect that was critical to the meaning of the metaphor. A common feeling amongst the validators, for example, is that the interpretation for *people who are terrorized by poverty* should include some mention of "fear" as a crucial aspect of the metaphor, as the interpretation provided states only that *"terrorize" implies that "poverty" is causing "people" not to function.* However, the end result of "fear" itself is often that the experiencer cannot function, as in *paralyzed by fear*.

Tables 4 and 5 contain interpretation system accuracy results by CM. We calculated the percentage of LMs evoking this CM that were validated as C vs. I (strict) or P/C vs. I (relaxed) by all three

	AgrS	AgrR	AccS ALL	AccS TWO	AccS ONE	AccR ALL	AccR TWO	AccR ONE
English	0.62	0.93	0.62	0.84	0.98	0.91	0.97	0.99
Russian	0.52	0.83	0.50	0.76	0.96	0.78	0.93	0.99

Table 3: Validation results for metaphor interpretation for English and Russian.

(ALL), or just two (TWO) validators. In most of the cases, the system performs well on "simple" CMs related to the concepts of causation and functioning (e.g., WEALTH is POWER), cf. section 4, whereas its accuracy is lower for richer metaphors (e.g., WEALTH is a GAME).

target	source	ALL		TWO	
		S	R	S	R
wealth	blood	0.8	1	1	1
	water	1	1	1	1
	drug	0.44	0.78	0.89	0.89
	food	0.89	1	1	1
	body	0.67	0.78	0.78	0.78
	power	1	1	1	1
	game	0.63	1	1	1
	security	0.14	0.88	0.71	1
	resource	1	1	1	1
	disease	0	1	1	1
poverty	war	0.9	0.9	1	1
	abyss	0	0.5	0.4	1
	violence	0	1	0.11	1
	price	0.88	0.88	0.88	1
	location	1	1	1	1
	disease	0.43	0.86	0.86	0.86
	crime	0.75	1	1	1
	crop	1	1	1	1
	terrorism	0	1	0.33	1
	cost	1	1	1	1

Table 4: Accuracy of English interpretations for each CM.

The data used in the described experiments, system output, and expert validations are available at *http://ovchinnikova.me/suppl/AbductionSystem-Metaphor-Validation.7z.*

6 Conclusion and Future Work

The developed abduction-based metaphor interpretation pipeline is available at *https://github.com/eovchinn/Metaphor-ADP* as a free open-source project. This pipeline produces favorable results, with metaphor interpretations that are rated as at least partially correct, for over 90% of all valid metaphors it is given for English, and close to 80% for Russian. Granted, the current research is performed using a small, controlled set of metaphors, so these results could prove difficult to reproduce on a large scale where any metaphor is possible. Still, the high accuracies achieved on both languages indicate

T	source	ALL		TWO	
		S	R	S	R
богатство (wealth)	энергия (energy)	0.4	0.8	0.9	1
	вода (water)	0	0.9	0.6	0.9
	свобода (freedom)	1	1	1	1
	власть (power)	1	1	1	1
	бог (god)	0.67	1	0.89	1
	кровь (blood)	1	1	1	1
	путь (way)	0.78	0.78	0.89	0.89
	игра (game)	0.1	0.2	0.2	0.3
	слава (glory)	0	0.75	0.75	1
	товар (ware)	0	0	0	1
бедность (poverty)	пропасть (abyss)	0.7	1	1	1
	враг (enemy)	0.56	1	1	1
	болезнь (disease)	0.33	0.89	0.67	1
	власть (power)	0.5	0.5	1	1
	тело (body)	0.17	0.17	0.17	0.83
	боль (pain)	1	1	1	1
	отчаяние (despair)	0.6	0.6	1	1
	цена (price)	0.75	0.75	1	1
	смерть (death)	0	0	0.33	1
	страх (fear)	0	1	0.67	1

Table 5: Accuracy of Russian interpretations for each CM.

that the approach is sound and there is potential for future work.

The current axiomatization methodology is based mainly on manually writing mapping axioms based on the axiom author's intuition. Obviously, this approach is subject to scrutiny regarding the appropriateness of the metaphors and faces scalability issues. Thus, developing new automatic methods to construct the domain knowledge bases is a main area for future consideration.

The mapping axioms present a significant challenge as far producing reliable output automatically. One area for consideration is the aforementioned prevalence of certain underlying meanings such as causality and functionality. Gathering enough examples of these by hand could lead to generalizations in argument structure that could then be applied to metaphorical phrases in corpora to extract new metaphors with similar meanings. Crowd-sourcing is another option that could be applied to both axiom writing tasks in order to develop a large-scale knowledge base in considerably less time and at a lower cost than having experts build the knowledge base manually.

References

R. Agerri, J.A. Barnden, M.G. Lee, and A.M. Wallington. 2007. Metaphor, inference and domain-independent mappings. In *Proc. of RANLP'07*, pages 17–23.

J. A. Barnden and M. G. Lee. 2002. An artificial intelligence approach to metaphor understanding. *Theoria et Historia Scientiarum*, 6(1):399–412.

M. Baroni and A. Lenci. 2008. Concepts and properties in word spaces. *Italian Journal of Linguistics*, 20(1):55–88.

J. Bos, S. Clark, M. Steedman, J. R. Curran, and J. Hockenmaier. 2004. Wide-coverage semantic representations from a ccg parser. In *Proc. of COLING'04*, pages 1240–1246.

P. Clark and P. Harrison. 2009. Large-scale extraction and use of knowledge from text. In *Proc. of the 5th international conference on Knowledge capture*, pages 153–160. ACM.

Catherine Havasi, Robert Speer, and Jason Alonso. 2007. Conceptnet 3: a flexible, multilingual semantic network for common sense knowledge. In *Recent Advances in Natural Language Processing*, Borovets, Bulgaria, September.

J. R. Hobbs, M. Stickel, P. Martin, and D. Edwards. 1993. Interpretation as abduction. *Artificial Intelligence*, 63:69–142.

J. R. Hobbs. 1985. Ontological promiscuity. In *Proc. of ACL*, pages 61–69, Chicago, Illinois.

J. R. Hobbs. 1992. Metaphor and abduction. In A. Ortony, J. Slack, and O. Stock, editors, *Communication from an Artificial Intelligence Perspective: Theoretical and Applied Issues*, pages 35–58. Springer, Berlin, Heidelberg.

Jerry R. Hobbs. 2005. Toward a useful concept of causality for lexical semantics. *Journal of Semantics*, 22(2):181–209.

N. Inoue and K. Inui. 2012. Large-scale cost-based abduction in full-fledged first-order predicate logic with cutting plane inference. In *Proc. of JELIA*, pages 281–293.

G. Lakoff and M. Johnson. 1980. *Metaphors we Live by*. University of Chicago Press.

G. Lakoff. 1987. *Women, fire, and dangerous things: what categories reveal about the mind*. University of Chicago Press.

S. Narayanan. 1999. Moving right along: A computational model of metaphoric reasoning about events. In *Proc. of AAAI/IAAI*, pages 121–127.

J. Nivre, J. Hall, and J. Nilsson. 2006. Maltparser: A data-driven parser-generator for dependency parsing. In *Proc. of LREC'06*, volume 6, pages 2216–2219.

R. Parker, D. Graff, J. Kong, K. Chen, and K. Maeda. 2011. English gigaword fifth edition. *LDC*.

A. Peñas and E. H. Hovy. 2010. Filling knowledge gaps in text for machine reading. In *Proc. of COLING'10*, pages 979–987.

S. Sharoff and J. Nivre. 2011. The proper place of men and machines in language technology: Processing Russian without any linguistic knowledge. In *Proc. Dialogue 2011, Russian Conference on Computational Linguistics*.

E. Shutova, T. Van de Cruys, and A. Korhonen. 2012. Unsupervised metaphor paraphrasing using a vector space model. In *COLING (Posters)*, pages 1121–1130.

E. Shutova. 2010. Automatic metaphor interpretation as a paraphrasing task. In *Proc. of NAACL'10*.

R. Speer and C. Havasi. 2013. Conceptnet 5: A large semantic network for relational knowledge. In *The People's Web Meets NLP*, pages 161–176. Springer.

N. Tsao and D. Wible. 2013. Word similarity using constructions as contextual features. In *Proc. JSSP'13*, pages 51–59.

T. Veale and Y. Hao. 2008. A fluid knowledge representation for understanding and generating creative metaphors. In *Proc. of COLING'08*, pages 945–952. ACL.

Computing Affect in Metaphors

Tomek Strzalkowski[1,2], Samira Shaikh[1], Kit Cho[1], George Aaron Broadwell[1], Laurie Feldman[1], Sarah Taylor[3], Boris Yamrom[1], Ting Liu[1], Ignacio Cases[1], Yuliya Peshkova[1] and Kyle Elliot[4]

[1]State University of New York - University at Albany
[2]Polish Academy of Sciences
[3]Sarah M. Taylor Consulting LLC
[4]Plessas Experts Network

tomek@albany.edu

Abstract

This article describes a novel approach to automated determination of affect associated with metaphorical language. Affect in language is understood to mean the attitude toward a topic that a writer attempts to convey to the reader by using a particular metaphor. This affect, which we will classify as positive, negative or neutral with various degrees of intensity, may arise from the target of the metaphor, from the choice of words used to describe it, or from other elements in its immediate linguistic context. We attempt to capture all these contributing elements in an Affect Calculus and demonstrate experimentally that the resulting method can accurately approximate human judgment. The work reported here is part of a larger effort to develop a highly accurate system for identifying, classifying, and comparing metaphors occurring in large volumes of text across four different languages: English, Spanish, Russian, and Farsi.

1 Introduction

We present an approach to identification and validation of affect in linguistic metaphors, i.e., metaphorical expressions occurring in written language. Our method is specifically aimed at isolating the affect conveyed in metaphors as opposed to more broad approaches to sentiment classification in the surrounding text. We demonstrate experimentally that our basic Affect Calculus captures metaphor-related affect with a high degree of accuracy when applied to neutral metaphor targets. These are targets that themselves do not carry any prior valuations. We subsequently expanded and refined this method to properly account for the contribution of the prior affect associated with the target as well as its immediate linguistic context.

2 Metaphor in Language

Metaphors are mapping systems that allow the semantics of a familiar Source domain to be applied to a new Target domain so as to invite new frameworks for reasoning (usually by analogy) to emerge in the target domain. The purpose of a metaphor is (a) to simplify or enable reasoning and communication about the target domain that would otherwise be difficult (because of technical complexity) or impossible (due to lack of agreed upon vocabulary) (e.g., Lakoff & Johnson, 1980; 2004); or (b) to frame the target domain in a particular way that enables one form of reasoning while inhibiting another (e.g., Thibodeau & Boroditsky, 2011). The two reasons for using metaphors are not necessarily mutually exclusive, in other words, (a) and (b) can operate at the same time. The distinction suggested above has to do with affect: a metaphor formed through (a) alone is likely to be neutral (e.g., client/server, messenger DNA), while a metaphor formed using (b) is likely to have a polarizing affect (e.g., tax's burden).

The Source and Target domains that serve as endpoints of a metaphoric mapping can be represented in a variety of ways; however, in a nutshell they are composed of two kinds of things: *concepts* and *relations*. In a Target domain the concepts are typically abstract, disembodied, often fuzzy concepts, such as *crime*, *mercy*, or *violence*, but may also include more concrete, novel, or elaborate concepts such as *democracy* or *economic inequality*. In a Source domain, the concepts are typically concrete and physical; however, mapping between two abstract domains is

Proceedings of the Second Workshop on Metaphor in NLP, pages 42–51,
Baltimore, MD, USA, 26 June 2014.

also possible. (E.g., *crime* may be both a target and a source domain.)

The *relations* of interest are those that operate between the concepts within a Source domain and can be "borrowed" to link concepts within the Target domain, e.g., "Crime$_{\text{(TARGET)}}$ *spread to*$_{\text{(RELATION)}}$ previously safe areas" may be borrowing from a DISEASE or a PARASITE source domain.

3 Related Research: metaphor detection

Most current research on metaphor falls into three groups: (1) theoretical linguistic approaches (as defined by Lakoff & Johnson, 1980; and their followers) that generally look at metaphors as abstract language constructs with complex semantic properties; (2) quantitative linguistic approaches (e.g., Charteris-Black, 2002; O'Halloran, 2007) that attempt to correlate metaphor semantics with their usage in naturally occurring text but generally lack robust tools to do so; and (3) social science approaches, particularly in psychology and anthropology that seek to explain how people produce and understand metaphors in interaction, but which lack the necessary computational tools to work with anything other than relatively isolated examples.

In computational investigations of metaphor, knowledge-based approaches include MetaBank (Martin, 1994), a large knowledge base of metaphors empirically collected. Krishnakumaran and Zhu (2007) use WordNet (Felbaum, 1998) knowledge to differentiate between metaphors and literal usage. Such approaches entail the existence of lexical resources that may not always be present or satisfactorily robust in different languages. Gedigan et al. (2006) identify a system that can recognize metaphor; however their approach is only shown to work in a narrow domain (*The Wall Street Journal*, for example).
Computational approaches to metaphor (largely AI research) to date have yielded only limited scale, often hand designed systems (Wilks, 1975; Fass, 1991; Martin, 1994; Carbonell, 1980; Feldman & Narayan, 2004; Shutova & Teufel, 2010; inter alia, also Shutova, 2010b for an overview). Baumer et al. (2010) used semantic role labels and typed dependency parsing in an attempt towards computational metaphor identification. However, they describe their own work as an initial exploration and hence, inconclusive. Shutova et al. (2010a) employ an unsupervised method of metaphor identification using nouns and verb clustering to automatically impute metaphoricity in a large corpus using an annotated training corpus of metaphors as seeds. Their method relies on annotated training data, which is difficult to produce in large quantities and may not be easily generated in different languages. Several other similar approaches were recently reported at the Meta4NLP [1] workshop, e.g., (Mohler et al., 2013; Wilks et al., 2013; Hovy et al., 2013).

Most recently, a significantly different approach to metaphor understanding based on lexical semantics and discourse analysis was introduced by Strzalkowski et al. (2013). Space constraints limit our discussion about their work in this article, however in the foregoing, our discussion is largely consistent with their framework.

4 Affect in Metaphors

Affect in language is understood to mean the attitude toward a topic that a speaker/writer attempts to convey to the reader or audience via text or speech (van der Sluis and Mellish 2008). It is expressed through multiple means, many of which are unrelated to metaphor. While affect in text is often associated, at least in theory, with a variety of basic emotions (anger, fear, etc.), it is generally possible to classify the set of possible affective states by polarity: positive, negative, and sometimes neutral. Affect is also considered to have a graded strength, sometimes referred to as intensity.

Our approach to affect in metaphor has been vetted not only by our core linguistic team but also by an independent team of linguist-analysts with whom we work to understand metaphor across several language-culture groups. Our research continues to show no difficulties in comprehension or disagreement across languages concerning the concept of linguistic affect, of its application to metaphor, and of its having both polarity and intensity.

5 Related Research: sentiment and affect

There is a relatively large volume of research on sentiment analysis in language (Kim and Hovy, 2004; Strapparava and Mihalcea, 2007; Wiebe and Cardie, 2005; inter alia) that aim at detecting polarity of text, but is not specifically concerned with metaphors. A number of systems were developed to automatically extract writer's senti-

[1] The First Workshop on Metaphor in NLP. http://aclweb.org/anthology//W/W13/W13-09.pdf

ment towards specific products or services such as movies or hotels, from online reviews (e.g., Turney, 2002; Pang and Lee, 2008) or social media messages (e.g., Thelwall et al., 2010). None of these techniques has been applied specifically to metaphorical language, and it is unclear if these alone would be sufficient due to the relatively complex semantics involved in metaphor interpretation. Socher et al. (2013 cite) have recently used recursive neural tensor networks to classify sentences into positive/negative categories. However, the presence of largely negative concepts such as "poverty" in a given sentence overwhelms the sentiment for the sentence in their method. Other relevant efforts in sentence level sentiment analysis include Sem-Eval Task[2]. While presence of affect in metaphorical language is well documented in linguistic and psycholinguistic literature (e.g., Osgood, 1980; Pavio and Walsh, 1993; Caffi and Janney, 1994; Steen, 1994), relatively little work was done to detect affect automatically. Some notable recent efforts include Zhang and Barnden (2010), Veale and Li (2012), and Kozareva (2013), who proposed various models of metaphor affect classification based primarily on lexical features of the surrounding text: specifically the word polarity information. In these and other similar approaches, which are closely related to sentiment analysis, affect is attributed to the entire text fragment: a sentence or utterance containing a metaphor, or in some cases the immediate textual context around it.

In contrast, our objective is to isolate affect due to the metaphor itself, independently of its particular context, and also to determine how various elements of the metaphoric expression contribute to its polarity and strength. For example, we may want to know what is the affect conveyed about the Government as a target concept of the metaphor in "*Government regulations are crushing small businesses*." and how it differs in "*Government programs help to eradicate poverty in rural areas*." or in "*Feds plan to raise the tax on the rich*." In all these examples, there is a subtle interplay between the prior affect associated with certain words (e.g., "*crush*", "*poverty*") and the semantic role they occupy in the sentence (e.g., agent vs. patient vs. location, etc.). Our objective is to develop an approach that can better explain such differences. Not surprisingly, in one of the target domains we are investigating, the Economic Inequality domain, there is considerable agreement on the basic attitudes across cultures towards the key target concepts: poverty is negative, wealth is positive, taxation is largely negative, and so on. This is in a marked contrast with another Target domain, the Governance domain where the target concepts tend to be neutral (e.g. bureaucracy, regulations etc.)

Another important motivation in developing our approach (although not discussed in this paper) is to obtain a model of affect that would help to explain empirically why metaphorically rich language is considered highly influential. Persuasion and influence literature (Soppory and Dillard, 2002) indicates messages containing metaphorical language produce somewhat greater attitude change than messages that do not. However, some recent studies (e.g., Broadwell et al., 2012) found that lexical models of affect, sentiment, or emotion in language do not correlate with established measures of influence, contrary to expectations. Therefore, a different approach to affect is needed based both on lexical and semantic features. We describe this new model below, and show some preliminary results in applications to metaphors interpretation.

6 Basic Affect Calculus

The need for a new approach to affect arises from the inability of the current methods of sentiment analysis to capture the affect that is conveyed by the metaphor itself, which may be only a part of the overall affect expressed in a text. Affect conveyed in metaphors, while often more polarized than in literal language, is achieved using subtler, less explicit, and more modulated expressions. This presents a challenge for NLP approaches that base affect determination upon the presence of explicit sentiment markers in language that may mask affect arising from a metaphor. This problem becomes more challenging when strong, explicit sentiment markers are present in a surrounding context or when the attitude of the speaker/writer towards the target concept is considered.

Our initial objective is thus to detect and classify the portion of affect that the speaker/writer is trying to convey by choosing a specific metaphor. The observables here are the linguistic metaphors that are actually uttered or written; therefore, our method must be able to determine affect present in the linguistic metaphors first and then extrapolate to the conceptual metaphor based on evidence across multiple uses of the

[2] https://www.cs.york.ac.uk/semeval-2013/task2/

same metaphor. Conceptual metaphors are posited by instances of linguistic metaphors that point to the same source domain. We choose initially to model the speaker/writer perspective; however, it may also be important to determine the effect that a metaphor has on the reader/listener, which we do not address here.

Affect in metaphor arises from the juxtaposition of a Source and a Target domain through the relations explicated in linguistic metaphors. These relations typically involve one or more predicates from the source domain that are applied to a target concept. For example, in "*Government regulations are crushing small businesses.*" the relation "*crushing*" is borrowed from a concrete source domain (e.g., Physical Burden), and used with an abstract target concept of "*government regulation*" which becomes the agentive argument, i.e., *crushed(GovReg, X)*, where *X* is an optional patientive argument, in this case "*small businesses*". Thus, government regulation is said to be doing something akin to "crushing", a harmful and negative activity according to the Affective Norms in English (ANEW) psycholinguistic database (Bradley and Lang, 1999). Since "government regulation" is doing something negative, the polarity of affect conveyed about it is also negative. The ANEW lexicon we are using contains ratings of ~100K words. The original ANEW lexicon by Bradley and Lang was expanded following the work done by Liu et al. (2014) in expanding the MRC imageability lexicon. While other sources of valence judgments exist such as NRC (Mohammad et al., 2013) and MPQA (Weibe and Cardie, 2005), there are limitations – for instance – NRC lexicon rates each words on a positive or negative scale, which does not allow for more fine-grained analysis of strength of valence.

Calculation from Table 1 is further generalized by incorporating the optional second argument of the relation and the role of the target concept (i.e., agentive or patientive). Thus, if *X*='small business' as in the example above, the complete relation becomes *crushed(GovReg, SmBus)*, which retains negative affect assuming that 'small business' is considered positive or at least neutral, an assessment that needs to be established independently.

The above calculations are captured in the Affect Calculus (AC), which was derived from the sociolinguistic models of topical positioning and disagreement in discourse (Broadwell et al., 2013).

The Affect Calculus was conceived as a hypothetical model of metaphorical affect, involving the metaphor target, the source relation, as well as the arguments of this relation, one of which is the target itself. The basic version of the AC is shown in Table 1. We should note that the AC allows us to make affect inferences about any of the elements of the metaphoric relation given the values of the remaining elements. We should also note that this calculus does not yet incorporate any discernable prior affect that the target concept itself may carry. When the target concept may be considered neutral (as is "government regulation" when taken out of context) this table allows us to compute the affect value of any linguistic metaphor containing it. This is unlike the target concepts such as "poverty" which bring their prior affect into the metaphor. We will return to this issue later.

In the Affect Calculus table, *Relation* denotes a unary or binary predicate (typically a verb, an adjective, or a noun). In the extended version of the AC (Section 6) *Relation* may also denote a compound consisting of a predicate and one or more *satellite arguments*, i.e., arguments other than AGENT or PATIENT, such as ORIGIN or DESTINATION for *motion verbs*, etc.

7 Extended Affect Calculus

The basic Affect Calculus does not incorporate any prior affect that the target concept might bring into a metaphor. This is fine in some domains (e.g., Government), where most target concepts may be considered neutral. But in other target domains, such as the Economic Inequality domain, many of the target concepts have a

Relation type	**Type 1 (propertive)** *Rel(Target)*	**Type 2 (agentive)** *Rel (Target, X)*		**Type 3 (patientive)** *Rel(X, Target)*	
Relation/X		$X \geq$ *neutral*	$X <$ *neutral*	$X \geq$ *neutral*	$X <$ *neutral*
Positive	POSITIVE	POSITIVE	≤ UNSYMP	POSITIVE	≤ SYMPAT
Negative	NEGATIVE	≤ UNSYMP	≥ SYMPAT	≤ SYMPAT	≥ SYMPAT
Neutral	NEUTRAL	NEUTRAL	≤ NEUTRAL	NEUTRAL	≤ NEUTRAL

Table 1. A simple affect calculus specifies affect polarity for linguistic metaphors using a 5-point polarity scale [negative < unsympathetic < neutral < sympathetic < positive]. X is the second argument.

strong prior affect in most cultures (e.g., 'poverty' is universally considered negative). We thus need to incorporate this prior affect into our calculation whenever an affect-loaded target concept is invoked in a metaphor. Where the basic Affect Calculus simply imposes a context-borne affect upon a neutral target concept, the Advanced Affect Calculus must combine it with the prior affect carried by the target concept, depending upon the type of semantic context. As already discussed, we differentiate 3 basic semantic contexts (and additional contexts in the extended Affect Calculus discussed in the next section) where the target concept is positioned with respect to other arguments in a metaphorical expression:

- *Propertive* context is when a property of a Target is specified (*e.g. deep poverty, sea of wealth*)
- *Agentive* context is when the Target appears as an agent of a relation that may involve another concept (Argument X) in the patient role (*e.g. Government regulations are crushing…, Government programs help…*)
- *Patientive* context is when the Target appears in the patient role that involves another concept (possibly implicit, Argument X) in the agent role. (*e.g. …eradicate poverty., ….navigate government bureaucracy)*

Table 1 (in the previous section) specifies how to calculate the affect expressed towards the target depending upon the affect associated with the Relation and the Argument X. In the Advanced Affect Calculus, this table specifies the *context-borne affect* that interacts with the affect associated with the target. When the target prior affect is unknown or assumed neutral, the AC table is applied directly, as explained previously. When the target has a known polarized affect, either positive or negative, the values in the AC table are used to calculate the final affect by combining the prior affect of the target with an appropriate value from the table. This is necessary for affect-loaded target concepts such as "poverty" or "wealth" that have strong prior affect and cannot be considered neutral.

In order to calculate the combined affect we define two operators ⊕ and ⊗. These operators form simple polarity algebra shown in Table 2. When the Target is in a Patientive relation, we use ⊗ to combine its affect with the context value from the AC table; otherwise, we use **⊕.** In the table for ⊕ operator, we note that combining opposing affects from the Target and the Relation causes the final affect to be undetermined (UND). In such cases we will take the affect of the stronger element (more polarized score) to prevail.

⊗	**pos**	**neg**	**neu**		**⊕**	**pos**	**neg**	**neu**
pos	pos	neg	pos		**pos**	pos	UND	pos
neg	neg	pos	neg		**neg**	UND	neg	neg
neu	pos	neg	neu		**neu**	pos	neg	neu

Table 2: Polarity algebra for extended affect calculus

More specifically, in order to determine the combined polarity score in these cases, we compute the distance between each element's ANEW score and the closest boundary of the neutral range of scores. For example, ANEW scores are assigned on a 10-point continuum (derived from human judgments on 10-point Likert scale) from most negative (0) to most positive (9). Values in the range of 3.0 to 5.0 may be considered neutral (this range can be set differently for target concepts and relations):

- Poverty affect score = 1.67 (ANEW) – 3 (neutral lower) = -1.33
- Grasp affect score = 5.45 (ANEW) – 5 (neutral upper)= +0.45

Consider the expression "poverty's grasp". Since poverty is a polarized target concept in Propertive position, we use ⊕ operator to combine its affect value with that of Relation (*grasp*). The result is negative:

- "Poverty's grasp" affect score (via AC⊕) = -1.33 + 0.45 = -0.82 (negative)

When the combined score is close to 0 (-0.5 to +0.5) the final affect is neutral.

7.1 Exceptions

The above calculus works in a majority of cases, but there are exceptions requiring specialized handling. An incomplete list of these is below (and cases will be added as we encounter them):

Reflexive relations. In some cases the target is in the agentive position but semantically it is also a patient, as in "poverty is spreading". These cases need to be handled carefully – although the current AC may be able to handle them in some contexts. When interpreted as an agentive relation, the affect of "poverty is spreading" comes out as undetermined but would likely be output as negative on the basis of the strong negative affect associated with poverty (vs. weaker positive affect of "spreading"). When handled as a patientive relation (an unknown force is spreading poverty), it comes out clearly and strongly negative. Similarly, "wealth is declining" is best handled through patientive relation. Therefore, for this AC we will treat intransitive relations as patientive.

Causative relations. Some relations denoted by causative verbs such as "alleviate", "mitigate" or "ease" appear to presuppose that their patient argument has negative affect, and their positive polarity already incorporates this assumption. Thus, "alleviate" is best interpreted as "reduce the negative of", which inserts an extra negation into the calculation. Without considering this extra negation we would calculate "alleviate(+) poverty(-)" as negative (doing something positive to a negative concept), which is not the expected reading. Therefore, the proposed special handling is to treat "alleviate" and similar relations as always producing positive affect when applied to negative targets.

8 Extensions to Basic Affect Calculus

The basic model presented in the preceding section oversimplifies certain more complex cases where the metaphoric relation involves more than 2 arguments. Consequently, we are considering several extensions to the basic Affect Calculus as suggested below. The foregoing should be treated as hypotheses subject to validation.

One possible extension involves relations represented by verbs of motion (which is a common source domain) that involve satellite arguments such as ORIGIN and DESTINATION in addition to the main AGENT and PATIENT roles. Any polarity associated with these arguments may impact affect directed at the target concept appearing in one of the main role positions. Likewise, we need a mechanism to calculate affect for target concepts found in one of the satellite roles. In "*Federal cuts could push millions into poverty*" the relation '*push into*' involves three arguments: AGENT (*Federal cuts*), PATIENT (*millions* [people]) and DESTINATION (*poverty*). In calculating affect towards 'Federal cuts' it is not sufficient to consider the polarity of the predicate "*push*" (or "*push into*"), but instead one must consider the polarity of "*push into (poverty)*" as the composite agentive relation involving 'federal cuts'. The polarity of this composite, in turn, depends upon the polarity of its destination argument. In other words:

polarity(*Rel*(DEST)) = *polarity* (DEST)

Thus, if '*poverty*' is negative, then pushing someone or something into poverty is a harmful relation. Assuming that '*millions* [people]' is considered at least neutral, we obtain negative affect for '*Federal cuts*' from the basic Affect Calculus table.

An analogous situation holds for the 'ORIGIN' argument, with the polarity reversed. Thus:

polarity (*Rel* (ORIGIN)) = ~*polarity* (ORIGIN)

In other words, the act of removing something from a bad place is helpful and positive. For example, in "*Higher retail wages would lift Americans out of poverty*" the relation compound "*lift out of (poverty)*" is considered helpful/positive. Again, once the polarity of the relation compound is established, the basic affect calculus applies as usual, thus we obtain positive affect towards '*higher retail wages*'. In situations when both arguments are present at the same time and point towards potentially conflicting outcomes, we shall establish a precedence order based on the evidence from human validation data.

Another class of multi-argument relations we are considering includes verbs that take an INSTRUMENT argument, typically signaled by '*with*' preposition. In this case, affect inference for the relation compound is postulated as follows:

polarity (*Rel* (INSTR))
= *polarity* (INSTR) if *polarity*(INSTR) < *neutral*
= *polarity* (*Rel*) otherwise

In other words, using a negative (bad) instrument always makes the relation harmful, while using a positive or neutral instrument has no effect on the base predicate polarity.

Other types of multi-argument relations may require similar treatment, and we are currently investigating further possible extensions. In all cases not explicitly covered in the extended Affect Calculus, we shall assume the default condition that other satellite arguments (such as TIME, LOCATION, etc.) will have no impact on the polarity of the source relation compound. In other words:

polarity (*Rel* (*s-role*)) $=_{\text{default}}$ *polarity* (*Rel*)

9 Evaluation and Results

For an evaluation, our objective is to construct a test that can evaluate the ability of an automated system to correctly identify and classify the affect associated with linguistic and conceptual metaphors. A series of naturally occurring text samples containing a linguistic metaphor about a target concept are presented as input to the system. The system outputs the affect associated with the metaphor, as positive, negative, or neutral. The system output is then compared to human generated answer key resulting in an accuracy score. The evaluation thus consists of two components:

1. Determining the ground truth about affect in test samples;
2. Measuring the automated system's ability to identify affect correctly.

Step 1 is done using human assessors who judge affect in a series of test samples. Assessors are presented with brief passages where a target concept and a relation are highlighted. They are asked to rank their responses on a 7-point scale for the following questions, among others:

- *To what degree does the above passage use metaphor to describe the highlighted concept?*
- *To what degree does this passage convey an idea that is either positive or negative?*

It is strictly necessary that input to the system be metaphorical sentences, since affect may be associated with non-metaphoric expressions as well; in fact, some direct expressions may carry stronger affect than subtle and indirect metaphors. This is why both questions on the survey are necessary: the first focuses the assessor's attention on the highlighted metaphor before asking about affect. If the purpose of the test is to measure the accuracy of assigning affect to a metaphor, then accuracy should be measured against the subset of expressions judged to be metaphorical.

The judgments collected from human assessors are tested for reliability and validity. Reliability among the raters is computed by measuring intra-class correlation (ICC) (McGraw & Wong, 1996; Shrout & Fleiss, 1979). Typically, a coefficient value above 0.7 indicates strong agreement. In general, our analyses have shown that we need approximately 30 or more subjects in order to obtain a reliability coefficient of at least 0.7. In addition, certain precautions were taken to ensure quality control in the data. We used the following criteria to discard a subject's data: (1) completed the task too quickly (i.e., averaged fewer than 10 seconds for each passage); (2) gave the same answer to 85% or more of the test items; (3) did not pass a simple language proficiency test; or (4) did not provide correct answers to a set of randomly inserted control passages which have been previously judged by experts to be unequivocally literal or metaphorical. Human judgments are collected using Amazon's Mechanical Turk services. For each passage in surveys, we would collect at least 30 viable judgments. In addition, we have native language speakers who have been rigorously trained to provide expert judgments on metaphor and affect identification task. Table 3 shows the intra-class correlations for affect determination amongst Mechanical Turk subjects. Experiments were conducted in 4 languages: English, Spanish, Russian, and Farsi.

	English	**Spanish**	**Russian**	**Farsi**
Metaphor	0.864	0.853	0.916	0.720
Affect	0.924	0.791	0.713	0.797

Table 3: Intra-class correlations for metaphor and affect assessment by Mechanical Turk subjects

In Figure 1, we present partial evidence that the human assessment collection method captures the phenomenon of affect associated with metaphors. The chart clearly shows that affect tends to be more polarized in metaphors than in literal expressions. The chart is based on more than 11,000 affect judgments for English linguistic metaphors and literal expressions about Governance concepts. We see a highly pronounced tendency towards the polarization of affect (both positive and negative). Ratings of affect (y-axis) in metaphoric expressions (columns 5-7) are judged to be stronger, and in particular more negative than the literal expressions (columns 1-3). A similar trend occurs with other target concepts as well as other languages, although the data are less reliable due to smaller test samples. Once an answer key is established using the aforementioned procedures, system accuracy can be determined from a confusion matrix as shown in Table 4. In Table 4, we show system assignment of affect versus answer key for English Governance and Economic Inequality target metaphors. Overall accuracy across positive, negative and neutral affect for English test set of 220 samples is 74.5%. Analogous confusion matrices have been constructed for Spanish, Russian and Farsi. NLP resources such as parser and lexicons for the languages other than English are not as robust or well rounded; therefore affect classification accuracy in those languages is impacted.

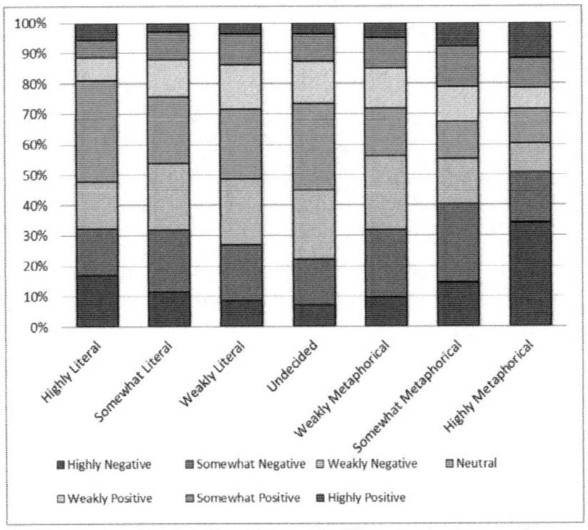

Figure 1: Distribution of affect polarity in human judgment of English literal and metaphorical expressions from the Governance domain. Metaphoricity of an expression (x-axis) is judged from highly literal (1) to highly metaphorical (7)

Table 5 shows the accuracy of affect detection for expressions that the system determined to be metaphors across all four languages under investigation. Evaluation set for numbers reported in Table 5 contains a total of 526 linguistic metaphors in these four languages.

English Affect Sample size = 220		System identified as		
		Positive	Negative	Neutral
Answer Key	Positive	40	16	3
	Negative	12	109	1
	Neutral	10	14	15

Table 4: Confusion matrix for affect classification in English linguistic metaphors in Governance and Economic Inequality Domain. Accuracy is 74.5%

	English	Spanish	Russian	Farsi
Accuracy	74.5%	71%	59%	64%

Table 5: Performance on affect classification for linguistic metaphors in four languages

10 Conclusion

In this paper we presented a new approach to automatic computing of affect in metaphors that exploits both lexical and semantic information in metaphorical expressions. Our method was evaluated through a series of rigorous experiments where more than several dozen of qualified assessors judged hundreds of sentences (extracted from online sources) that contained metaphorical expressions. The objective was to capture affect associated with the metaphor itself. Our system can approximate human judgment with accuracy ranging from 59% for Russian to 74% for English. These results are quite promising. The differences are primarily due to varied robustness of the language processing tools (such as parsers and morphological analyzers) that are available for each language. We note that a direct comparison to lexical approaches such as described by Kozareva (2013) is not possible at this time due to differences in assessment methodology, although it remains one of our objectives.

Our next step is to demonstrate that the new way of calculating affect can lead to a reliable model of affective language use that correlates with other established measures of influence.

Acknowledgements

Supported by the Intelligence Advanced Research Projects Activity (IARPA) via Department of Defense US Army Research Laboratory contract number W911NF-12-C-0024. The U.S. Government is authorized to reproduce and distribute reprints for Governmental purposes notwithstanding any copyright annotation thereon. Disclaimer: The views and conclusions contained herein are those of the authors and should not be interpreted as necessarily representing the official policies or endorsements, either expressed or implied, of IARPA, DoD/ARL, or the U.S. Government.

References

David W. Allbritton, Gail McKoon, and Richard J. Gerrig. 1995. Metaphor-based schemas and text Representations: making connections through conceptual metaphors, *Journal of Experimental Psychology: Learning, Memory, and Cognition*, 21(3):612-625.

Eric P. S. Baumer, James P. White, and Bill Tomlinson. 2010. Comparing semantic role labeling with typed dependency parsing in computational metaphor identification. In *Proceedings of the NAACL HLT 2010 Second Workshop on Computational Approaches to Linguistic Creativity*, pages 14–22, Los Angeles, California.

Margaret M. Bradley, and Peter Lang. 1999. Affective norms for English words (ANEW): Instruction manual and affective ratings. Technical Report C-2. University of Florida, Gainesville, FL.

George Aaron Broadwell, Umit Boz, Ignacio Cases, Tomek Strzalkowski, Laurie Feldman, Sarah Taylor, Samira Shaikh, Ting Liu, Kit Cho, and Nick Webb. 2013. Using imageability and topic chaining to locate metaphors in linguistic corpora. In *Proceedings of International Conference on Social Computing, Behavioral-Cultural Modeling, & Prediction*, pages 102–109. Washington D.C.

George Aaron Broadwell, Jennifer Stromer-Galley, Tomek Strzalkowski, Samira Shaikh, Sarah Taylor, Umit Boz, Alana Elia, Laura Jiao, Ting Liu and Nick Webb. 2012. Modeling socio-cultural phenomena in discourse. *Journal of Natural Language Engineering*, pages 1–45. *Cambridge Press.*

Claudia Caffi, and Richard W. Janney. 1994. Towards a pragmatics of emotive communication. *Journal of Pragmatics*, 22:325–373.

Jaime Carbonell. 1980. Metaphor: A key to extensible semantic analysis. In *Proceedings of the 18th Annual Meeting on Association for Computational Linguistics*.

Jonathan, Charteris-Black. 2002. Second language figurative proficiency: A comparative study of Malay and English. *Applied Linguistics* 23(1):104–133.

Dan, Fass. 1991. met*: A Method for Discriminating Metonymy and Metaphor by Computer. *Computational Linguistics*, 17:49-90

Jerome Feldman, and Srinivas Narayanan. 2004. Embodied meaning in a neural theory of language. *Brain and Language*, 89(2):385–392.

Christiane D. Fellbaum. 1998. *WordNet: An electronic lexical database* (1st ed.). MIT Press.

Matt Gedigian, John Bryant, Srini Narayanan and Branimir Ciric. 2006. Catching Metaphors. In *Proceedings of the Third Workshop on Scalable Natural Language Understanding ScaNaLU 2006*, pages 41–48. New York City: NY.

Dirk Hovy, Shashank Shrivastava, Sujay Kumar Jauhar, Mrinmaya Sachan, Kartik Goyal, Huying Li, Whitney Sanders and Eduard Hovy. 2013. Identifying Metaphorical Word Use with Tree Kernels. In the *Proceedings of the First Workshop on Metaphor in NLP, (NAACL)*. Atlanta.

Soo-Min Kim and Eduard Hovy. 2004. Determining the sentiment of opinions. In *Proceedings of the 20th international conference on Computational Linguistics*, COLING '04.

Zornitsa Kozareva. 2013. Multilingual Affect Polarity and Valence Prediction in Metaphor-Rich Texts. In *Proceedings of the 51st Annual Meeting of the Association for Computational Linguistics* (ACL 2013)

Saisuresh Krishnakumaran and Xiaojin Zhu. 2007. Hunting elusive metaphors using lexical resources. In *Proceedings of the Workshop on Computational Approaches to Figurative Language*, pages 13–20. Rochester, NY.

George Lakoff, and Mark Johnson. 1980. *Metaphors we live by*. University Of Chicago Press, Chicago, Illinois.

George, Lakoff. 2001. *Moral politics: what conservatives know that liberals don't.* University of Chicago Press, Chicago, Illinois.

Ting Liu, Kit Cho, George Aaron Broadwell, Samira Shaikh, Tomek Strzalkowski, John Lien, Sarah Taylor, Laurie Feldman, Boris Yamrom, Nick Webb, Umit Boz and Ignacio Cases. 2014. Automatic Expansion of the MRC Psycholinguistic Database Imageability Ratings. In Proceedings of *9th Language Resources and Evaluation Conference*, (LREC 2014)Reykjavik, Iceland.

Liisa, Malkki. 1992. National geographic: The rooting of people and the territorialization of national identity among scholars and refugees. *Society for Cultural Anthropology*, 7(1):24–44.

James Martin. 1988. A computational theory of metaphor. *Ph.D. Dissertation.*

Kenneth O. McGraw and S. P. Wong. 1996. Forming inferences about some intraclass correlation coefficients. *Psychological Methods, 1*(1): 30–46.

Mohammad, S.M., S. Kiritchenko, and X. Zhu. 2013. NRC-Canada: Building the state-of-the-art insentiment analysis of tweets. In Proceedings of the *Seventh International Workshop on Semantic Evaluation Exercises* (SemEval-2013), Atlanta, Georgia, USA, June 2013.

Michael Mohler, David Bracewell, David Hinote, and Marc Tomlinson. 2013. Semantic signatures for example-based linguistic metaphor detection. In The *Proceedings of the First Workshop on Metaphor in NLP, (NAACL)*, pages 46–54.

Musolff, Andreas. 2008. What can critical metaphor analysis add to the understanding of racist ideology? Recent studies of Hitler's anti-semitic metaphors, critical approaches to discourse analysis across disciplines. Critical *Approaches to Discourse Analysis Across Disciplines*, 2(2):1–10.

Kieran, O'Halloran. 2007. Critical discourse analysis and the corpus-informed interpretation of metaphor at the register level. *Oxford University Press*

Charles E. Osgood. 1981. The cognitive dynamics of synaesthesia and metaphor. In *Proceedings of the National Symposium for Research in Art. Learning in Art: Representation and Metaphor*, pages 56-80. University of Illinois Press.

Bo Pang and Lillian Lee. 2008. Opinion mining and sentiment analysis. Found. *Trends Inf. Retr.*, 2(1-2):1–135, January.

Allan Pavio and Mary Walsh. 1993. Psychological processes in metaphor comprehension and memory. In Andrew Ortony, editor, *Metaphor and thought* (2nd ed.). Cambridge: Cambridge University Press.

Patrick E Shrout and Joseph L Fleiss. 1979. Intraclass correlations: Uses in assessing rater reliability. *Psychological Bulletin, 86*(2):420–428.

Ekaterina Shutova. 2010. Models of metaphors in NLP. In *Proceedings of ACL 2010. Uppsala, Sweden.*

Ekaterina Shutova and Simone Teufel. 2010a. Metaphor corpus annotated for source - target domain mappings. *In Proceedings of Language Resources and Evaluation Conference 2010*. Malta.

Ekaterina Shutova. 2010b. Models of metaphor in nlp. In *Proceedings of the 48th Annual Meeting of the Association for Computational Linguistics*, ACL '10, pages 688–697.

Ekaterina Shutova, Tim Van de Cruys, and Anna Korhonen. 2012. *Unsupervised metaphor paraphrasing using a vector space model* In *Proceedings of COLING 2012*, Mumbai, India

Richard Socher, Alex Perelygin, Jean Wu, Jason Chuang, Chris Manning, Andrew Ng and Chris Potts. 2013. In *Proceedings Conference on Empirical Methods in Natural Language Processing* (EMNLP 2013). Seattle, USA.

Sopory, P. and Dillard, J. P. (2002), The Persuasive Effects of Metaphor: A Meta-Analysis. Human Communication Research, 28: 382–419. doi: 10.1111/j.1468-2958.2002.tb00813.x

Gerard Steen. 1994. Understanding metaphor in literature: An empirical approach. London: Longman.

Carlo, Strapparava, and Rada Mihalcea. 2007. Semeval-2007 task 14: Affective text. In *Proceedings of the Fourth International Workshop on Semantic Evaluations*, pages 70–74. Association for Computational Linguistics.

Tomek Strzalkowski, George Aaron Broadwell, Sarah Taylor, Laurie Feldman, Boris Yamrom, Samira Shaikh, Ting Liu, Kit Cho, Umit Boz, Ignacio Cases and Kyle Elliott. 2013. Robust extraction of metaphor from novel data. In *Proceedings of Workshop on Metaphor in NLP, NAACL*. Atlanta.

Mike Thelwall, Kevan Buckley, and Georgios Paltoglou. Sentiment in Twitter events. 2011. Journal of the American Society for Information Science and Technology, 62(2):406–418.

Paul H. Thibodeau and Lera Boroditsky. 2011. Metaphors We Think With: The Role of Metaphor in Reasoning. *PLoS ONE* 6(2): e16782.

Peter D, Turney. 2002. Thumbs up or thumbs down? Semantic orientation applied to unsupervised classification of reviews. In *Proceedings of the 40th Annual Meeting on Association for Computational Linguistics, ACL '02*, pages 417–424.

Ielka van der Sluis, and C. Mellish 2008. Toward affective natural language deneration: Empirical investigations. affective language in human and machine. AISB 2008 Proceedings Volume 2.

Tony Veale and Guofu Li. 2012. Specifying viewpoint and information need with affective metaphors: a system demonstration of the metaphor magnet web app/service. In *Proceedings of the ACL 2012 System Demonstrations*, ACL '12, pages 7–12.

Janyce, Wiebe and Claire Cardie. 2005. Annotating expressions of opinions and emotions in language. In *Language Resources and Evaluation*.

Yorick, Wilks. 1975. Preference semantics. *Formal Semantics of Natural Language*, E. L. Keenan, Ed. Cambridge University Press, Cambridge, U.K., 329–348.

Yorick Wilks, Lucian Galescu, James Allen, Adam Dalton. 2013. Automatic Metaphor Detection using Large-Scale Lexical Resources and Conventional Metaphor Extraction. In the *Proceedings of the First Workshop on Metaphor in NLP, (NAACL)*. Atlanta.

Wiebe, J., Wilson, T., and Cardie, C.: Annotating expressions of opinions and emotions in language. *Language Resources and Evaluation*, 39(2-3), pp. 165-210 (2005).

Li Zhang and John Barnden. 2010. Affect and metaphor sensing in virtual drama. International Journal of Computer Games Technology. Vol. 2010.

A Service-Oriented Architecture for Metaphor Processing

Tony Veale
School of Computer Science and Informatics
University College Dublin
Belfield, Dublin D4, Ireland.
Tony.Veale@UCD.ie

Abstract

Metaphor is much more than a pyrotechnical flourish of language or a fascinating conceptual puzzle: it is a cognitive *lever* that allows speakers to leverage their knowledge of one domain to describe, reframe and understand another. Though NLP researchers tend to view metaphor as a problem to be solved, metaphor is perhaps more fittingly seen as a *solution* to be used, that is, as an important tool in the support of creative thinking and the generation of diverse linguistic outputs. Since it pays to think of metaphor as a foundational cognitive service, one that can be exploited in a wide array of creative computational tasks, we present here a view of metaphor as a public *Web service* that can be freely called on demand.

1 Introduction

Metaphor is a knowledge-hungry phenomenon. Fortunately, much of the knowledge needed for the processing of metaphor is already implicit in the large body of metaphors that are active in a language community (e.g. Martin, 1990; Mason, 2004). For existing metaphors are themselves a valuable source of knowledge for the production of new metaphors, so much so that a system can mine the relevant knowledge from corpora of figurative text (see Veale, 2011; Shutova, 2010). Thus, though linguistic metaphors are most naturally viewed as the output of a language generation process, and as the input to a language understanding process, it is just as meaningful to view the conceptual metaphors that underpin these linguistic forms as an *input* to the generation process and an *output* of the understanding process. A rich source of existing linguistic metaphors, such as a text corpus or a database of Web n-grams, can thus be viewed as an implicit source of the knowledge a system needs to generate and understand novel linguistic metaphors. Of course, if one finds Web data to be a useful resource for metaphor, it also makes sense to think of the algorithms and tools for manipulating this knowledge as Web *services*, online systems that hide the complexity of metaphor processing yet which can be called upon to generate and understand linguistic metaphors on demand. Such metaphors can then, in turn, be exploited in higher-level linguistic outputs such as stories and poems by yet other, inter-operable Web services.

There are compelling reasons to see metaphor as a service rather than a problem. For one, many creative language tasks – such as poetry, joke and story generation – require the conceptual and linguistic divergence offered by metaphor. When metaphor is offered as a reusable Web service, such systems need not implement their own metaphor solutions, and are instead freed to focus on providing their own unique competences. For another, even as a problem, metaphor is not yet a *standardized* problem in NLP, and so different researchers focus on diverse aspects of metaphor using a wide range of bespoke models and approaches. But when these models are provided as public services, researchers are free to draw from a rich ecology of complementary solutions. New approaches to metaphor, and to broader problems of linguistic creativity, may then emerge as researchers and developers mix-and-match services to meet their own specific application needs.

A *Service-Oriented Architecture*, or SOA, is one in which solution logic is presented in the form of discoverable, modular and composable services that hide the complexity of their data and their inner workings (Erl, 2008). This paper advocates for a SOA treatment of metaphor in the form of open and reusable Web services. To this end, a number of metaphor Web services are

Proceedings of the Second Workshop on Metaphor in NLP, pages 52–60,
Baltimore, MD, USA, 26 June 2014.

presented, to both offer a practical demonstration of the merits of SOA and to kick-start further development of metaphor services by the field. After discussing related work in section 2, we thus present a series of publically-accessible metaphor services, for generating creative similes, for performing divergent categorization, for generating new affective metaphors from old, for generating metaphor-rich poetry, and for generating metaphor-inspired character arcs for stories.

2 Related Work and Ideas

Metaphor has been studied within computer science for four decades, yet it remains largely at the periphery of NLP research. The reasons for this marginalization are pragmatic ones, since metaphors can be as challenging as human creativity will allow. The greatest success has thus been achieved by focusing on conventional metaphors (e.g., Martin, 1990; Mason, 2004), or on specific domains of usage, such as figurative descriptions of mental states (e.g., Barnden, 2006).

From the earliest computational forays, it has been recognized that metaphor is fundamentally a problem of knowledge representation. Semantic representations are, by and large, designed for well-behaved mappings of words to meanings – what Hanks (2006) calls *norms* – but metaphor requires a system of soft preferences rather than hard (and brittle) constraints. Wilks (1978) thus proposed a *preference semantics* approach, which Fass (1991,1997) extended into a *collative semantics*. In contrast, Way (1990) argued that metaphor requires a dynamic concept hierarchy that can stretch to meet the norm-bending demands of figurative ideation, though her approach lacked specific computational substance.

More recently, some success has been obtained with statistical approaches that side-step the problems of knowledge representation, by working instead with implied or latent representations that are derived from word distributions. Turney and Littman (2005) show how a statistical model of relational similarity that is constructed from Web texts can retrieve the correct answers for proportional analogies, of the kind used in SAT/GRE tests. No hand-coded knowledge is employed, yet Turney and Littman's system achieves an average human grade on a set of 376 real SAT analogies.

Shutova (2010) annotates verbal metaphors in corpora (such as "to *stir* excitement", where "stir" is used metaphorically) with the corresponding conceptual metaphors identified by Lakoff and Johnson (1980). Statistical clustering techniques are then used to generalize from the annotated exemplars, allowing the system to recognize and retrieve other metaphors in the same vein (e.g. "he *swallowed* his anger"). These clusters can also be analyzed to find literal paraphrases for a given metaphor (e.g. "to *provoke* excitement" or "*suppress* anger"). Shutova's approach is noteworthy for operating with Lakoff and Johnson's inventory of conceptual metaphors without using an explicit knowledge representation of the knowledge domains involved.

Hanks (2006) argues that metaphors exploit distributional norms: to understand a metaphor, one must first recognize the norm that is exploited. Common norms in language are the preferred semantic arguments of verbs, as well as idioms, clichés and other multi-word expressions. Veale and Hao (2007a) suggest that stereotypes are conceptual norms that are found in many figurative expressions, and note that stereotypes and similes enjoy a symbiotic relationship that has obvious computational advantages. Similes rely on stereotypes to illustrate the qualities ascribed to a topic, while stereotypes are often promulgated via proverbial similes (Taylor, 1954). Veale and Hao (2007a) show how stereotypical knowledge can be acquired by harvesting "Hearst" patterns (Hearst, 1992) of the form "as P as C" (e.g. "*as smooth as silk*") from the Web. They go on to show in (2007b) how this body of stereotypes can be used in a Web-based model of metaphor generation and comprehension.

Veale (2011) employs stereotypes as the basis of the *Creative Information Retrieval* paradigm, by introducing a variety of non-literal-matching wildcards in the vein of Mihalcea (2002). In this paradigm, **@Noun** matches any adjective that denotes a stereotypical property of *Noun* (so e.g. ***@knife*** matches *sharp, pointy*, etc.) while **@Adj** matches any noun for which *Adj* is stereotypical (e.g. ***@sharp*** matches *sword, laser, razor*, etc.). In addition, **?Adj** matches any property / behavior that co-occurs with, and reinforces, the property denoted by *Adj* in similes; thus, ***?hot*** matches *humid, sultry* and *spicy*. Likewise, **?Noun** matches any noun that denotes a pragmatic neighbor of *Noun*, where two words are neighbors if corpora attest to the fact that they are often clustered together as comparable ideas, as in "*lawyers and doctors*" or "*pirates and thieves*". The knowledge needed for @ is obtained by harvesting text from the Web, while that for **?** is obtained by mining Google 3-grams for instances of the form "*Xs and Ys*" (Brants and Franz 2006).

Creative Information Retrieval (CIR) can be used as a platform for the design of many Web services that offer linguistic creativity on demand. By enabling the flexible retrieval of n-gram data for non-literal queries, CIR allows a wide variety of creative tasks to be reimagined as simple IR tasks (Veale 2013). In the next section we show how CIR facilitates the generation of creative similes from linguistic readymades.

3 The Jigsaw Bard

Similes and stereotypes enjoy a mutually beneficial relationship. Stereotypes anchor our similes in familiar concepts with obvious features, while similes, for their part, further popularize these stereotypes and entrench them in a culture. Since the core of any good simile is an evocative stereotype that embodies just the qualities we want to communicate (see Fishelov, 1992), simile generation is essentially a problem of apt stereotype retrieval. However, we can also turn this view on its head by asking: what kinds of simile might be generated from a given stereotype, or a linguistic combination or two or more lexicalized stereotypes? For instance, were we to consider the many phrases in the Google n-grams that combine a lexicalized stereotype with an affective modifier (such as "*cold fish*"), or that combine multiple stereotypes with shared qualities (such as "*chocolate espresso*" (brown) or "*robot fish*" (cold and emotionless)), we might imagine re-purposing these phrases as part of a novel simile such as "*as emotionless as a robot fish*" or perhaps even "*as smooth as a chocolate martini*".

The n-grams encountered and re-purposed in this way are linguistic *readymades*, in much the same way that the everyday objects that catch an artist's eye for their secondary aesthetic qualities become art when re-imagined as art (see Taylor, 2009). Readymades in art are a product of serendipity: an artist encounters an object – perhaps a humble tool, or the discarded detritus of modern life – and sees in it a desired quality that can be brought to the fore in the right setting. Using a computer, however, linguistic readymades can be harvested from a resource like the Google n-grams on a near-industrial scale. Using CIR, a query can be issued for all bigrams that combine a lexicalized stereotype with a modifier that accentuates one of the stereotype's core qualities. Such a query might be "?@P @P" where P denotes a property like *cold* or *smooth*; the CIR query "?@cold @cold" thus matches "*wet fish*". Likewise, a CIR query of the form "@P @P" will retrieve all Google bigrams that juxtapose two lexicalized stereotypes for the same property P; thus, "@cold @cold" retrieves "*January rain*", "*winter snow*" and "*robot fish*". More elaborate queries will retrieve more elaborate n-grams, such as "*snow-covered grave*" and "*bullet-riddled corpse*" (again for the property *cold*).

The *Jigsaw Bard* is a creative Web service that exploits this notion of linguistic readymades to generate novel creative similes on demand. Of course, the Bard only appears to "invent" similes on demand (for a given input property like *cold*). In fact, the Bard has already scanned all of the Google n-grams to index a great many potential readymades that may, for some future request, be re-purposed as a creative simile. In keeping with the principles of SOA, the *Bard* does as little processing in real time as possible. Thus, when called as a Web service, it reliably retrieves, with remarkable speed, scores of fascinating similes that have already been indexed for a property. The *Jigsaw Bard* service can be accessed online at: *www.educatedinsolence.com/jigsaw/*

4 Thesaurus Rex

Metaphor is both a viewfinder and an adjustable lens: it helps us to find distant objects that share surprising similarities, and it allows us to focus on shared qualities that are not always apparent in a more conventional setting. So while metaphor exploits our sense of similarity to generate resonant yet surprising juxtapositions, it also *directs* our sense of similarity, to highlight shared qualities that might otherwise remain unnoticed.

One cannot have an eye for metaphor without also having a well-developed sense of similarity. Lexico-semantic resources like WordNet offer NLP researchers a comprehensive and widely-used basis for measuring the similarity of two words or lexical concepts (see Fellbaum, 1998). Yet WordNet offers a somewhat monochromatic view of conceptual structure: it is a convergent structure in which every lexical concept is put in its correct place according to conventional usage. Metaphor requires a more kaleidoscopic view of conceptual structure, in which the many diverse and unconventional ways that a word, object or idea may be used can be brought into play. The best place to find this kind of divergence is not a carefully curated resource like WordNet, but the unfiltered clamor and eclecticism of the Web.

One can see the many ways in a given lexical concept is viewed on the Web using a simple search query. The "such" construction, as used in "*expensive foods such as lobster and caviar*", tells us that lobster and caviar are seen by some as expensive foods. The more often this view is found on the Web, the more credibility it can be given. Yet rather than trawl the Web for all uses of the "such" construction, it pays to be targeted and parsimonious in our searches. For instance, suppose a system already possesses the stereotypical association that *Champagne* is *expensive*. A targeted query of the form "*expensive * such as * and Champagne*" will now retrieve Web texts that indicate other, related expensive items, and an umbrella category in which to place them all. Google, for example, provides the snippets "*expensive wines such as French Burgundy and Champagne*", "*expensive products such as Cognac and Champagne*" and "*expensive and exotic foodstuffs such as caviar, seafood, hares, game, wine and champagne*" in response to this query.

Knowing that *Champagne* and *caviar* are expensive items in the same category, a system can now look for the other categories they also share, and so the query "*expensive * such as caviar and Champagne*" finds that they are also considered to be *expensive delicacies* on the Web. By starting from a small seed of stereotypical knowledge (e.g. that *Champagne* is *expensive*), a system can generate a large body of targeted Web queries to elaborate and expand this knowledge. As new qualities and nuanced categories are acquired, these too can feed into the targeted acquisition process to form a virtuous bootstrapping circle.

As a result, a system that starts from a seed of 12,000 or so stereotypical associations will acquire over 1.5 million fine-grained categorizations in just five cycles of bootstrapping. Thus, for instance, a system can view *Champagne* as more than just a food, as the Web snippet "*luxury goods such as diamonds and champagne*" can attest. These many fine-grained, overlapping and competing perspectives – when combined in a Web service for divergent categorization we call *Thesaurus Rex* – provide the kaleidoscopic swirl of possibilities that WordNet is so lacking but which creative metaphors can do so much with.

Ask WordNet what the lexicalized concepts *War* and *Peace*, or *Life* and *Death*, or *Divorce* and *War* have in common, and its answer cannot fail but to disappoint. WordNet simply does not possess the fine-grained category structure to suggest what features might be shared by these very different concepts, even if, ironically, it can be used to generate a meaningful-seeming *numerical* measure of similarity in each case. In contrast, the *Thesaurus Rex* Web service will return a wealth of informative commonalities in each case. For instance, Figure 1 below presents a phrase cloud of the nuanced categories that are shared by both *War* and *Divorce*. Note how each is categorized as a stressful event, an unexpected and dramatic event, a traumatic event and an emotional event (eagle-eyed readers will note that each is also an adverse economic event).

Figure 1. Shared categories for *War* and *Divorce*.

Thesaurus Rex thus provides a valuable service to any system that wishes to take a divergent view of conceptual structure, whether for purposes of literal similarity assessment or for non-literal metaphoric reasoning. *Rex* can be used as a browsing tool by Web users in search of insights or apt comparisons – for instance, one can go from *Leadership* to *Creativity* via the categories *soft skill*, *valuable skill* or *transferable skill* – or as a flexible similarity service that supports 3rd-party metaphor processing systems. It should be noted that while *Rex* relies on the Web for its divergent view of the world, it does not sacrifice quality for quantity. Veale & Li (2013) show that a combination of *Thesaurus Rex* and WordNet produces similarity scores for the standard Miller & Charles (1991) test-set that achieve a 0.93 correlation with human judgments. This is as good as the best machine-learning systems (which do not *explain* their ratings the way that *Rex* can) and far superior to any WordNet-only approach. The Thesaurus Rex service can be accessed here:

http://boundinanutshell.com/therex2

5 Metaphor Magnet

In many ways, a metaphor resembles a query in information retrieval (IR). Metaphors, like queries, allow us to simultaneously express what we believe and to elicit further information that may bolster or refute our beliefs. Metaphors, like queries, are often short and concise, and require unpacking and expansion to be properly understood and acted upon. An expanded IR query is considered successful if it leads to the retrieval of a richer set of relevant information sources. Likewise, an expanded metaphor can be considered successful if expansion produces a rich interpretation that is consonant with, and consistently adds to, our beliefs about a particular topic.

Of course, there are important differences between metaphors, which elicit information from other humans, and IR queries, which elicit information from search engines. For one, IR fails to discriminate literal from non-literal language (see Veale 2004, 2011), and reduces any metaphoric query to literal keywords and key-phrases that are matched near-identically to texts (see Salton, 1968; Van Rijsbergen 1979). Yet everyday language shows that metaphor is an ideal form for expressing our information needs. A query like "*Steve Jobs was a good leader*", say, can be viewed by a creative IR system as a request to consider all the ways in which leaders are typically good, and to then consider all the metaphors that can most appropriately be used to convey these viewpoints about *Steve Jobs*.

IR techniques such as corpus-based query expansion can thus be used to understand and generate metaphors on demand, if IR staples like query expansion (see Vorhees, 1998; Navigli and Velardi, 2003) are made both *affect-driven* and *metaphor-aware*. Expansion in each case can be performed using a comprehensive database of affective stereotypes that indicate e.g. the stereotypical properties of *geniuses*, *gurus* and *tyrants*.

Let us return to the example of Steve Jobs *qua* leader. Using the CIR query "leader is a ?leader" a range of different kinds of leader can be retrieved. For instance, the Google n-grams oblige with the 4-grams "leader is a *visionary*", "leader is a *tyrant*", "leader is a *terrorist*", "leader is a *master*", "leader is a *shepherd*", "leader is a *dictator*", "leader is an *expert*", "leader is a *teacher*" and "leader is a *catalyst*". But which of these views is consonant with being a *good* leader? If one wanted to criticize Jobs' leadership of Apple, then the stereotypes *tyrant*, *terrorist* and *dictator* offer clearly negative perspectives. In contrast, the stereotypes *visionary*, *shepherd, expert* and *teacher* are all positive, while *master* and *catalyst* may each evoke both good and bad qualities.

The under-specified positive metaphor "Steve Jobs was a *good* leader" can thus be expanded, via the Google n-grams, to generate the specific positive metaphors "Steve Jobs was a *visionary*", "Steve Jobs was a *shepherd*", "Steve Jobs was an *expert*" and "Steve Jobs was a *teacher*". Likewise, the under-specified negative metaphor "Steve Jobs was a *bad* leader" can be expanded to yield "Steve Jobs was a *tyrant*", "Steve Jobs was a *dictator*" and "Steve Jobs was a *terrorist*". The stereotypical properties of the vehicle in each case – such as *tyrant* or *expert* – can then be projected onto the tenor, Steve *Jobs* qua leader. Which properties of the vehicle are most relevant to Steve Jobs as a leader? CIR is again used to rank properties by their relevance to leadership. For instance, the CIR query "@tyrant leader" finds Google 2-grams where a property of *tyrant* is used to describe a leader – such as "*cruel leader*" and "*demanding leader*" – and allows a system to rank the properties of *tyrant* according to the frequencies of these corresponding 2-grams.

Metaphor Magnet is such a system. Deployed as a Web service that generates and expands affective metaphors on demand, *Metaphor Magnet* allows clients (human users or 3rd-party software systems) to enter single terms (such as *leader*), compound terms with an affective spin (such as *good leader* or *+leader*), or copula statements such as "*Steve Jobs is a +leader*". For each input, the service marries its extensive knowledge of lexicalized stereotypes to the grand scale of the Google n-grams, to meaningfully expand upon what it has been given and to generate the most appropriate affective elaborations and interpretations it can muster. In each case, *Metaphor Magnet* provides a rich property-level explanation of its outputs. So, for instance, if Steve Jobs were to be viewed as a *master*, the properties *skilled*, *enlightened*, *free* and *demanding* are all highlighted as being most appropriate. The Metaphor Magnet service can be accessed here:

http://boundinanutshell.com/metaphor-magnet-acl

6 Metaphorize with Metaphor Eyes

Metaphor Magnet offers a property-theoretic view of metaphor: since its model of the world is entirely property-based – in which words denote stereotypes that map to highly salient properties – it sees metaphor interpretation as a question of which properties are mapped from the vehicle to the tenor. *Metaphor Magnet* lacks a proposition-level view of the world, in which stereotypes are linked to other stereotypes by arbitrary relations. Thus, though it knows that *scientists* are *logical* and *objective*, it does not know, and cannot use, the generalizations that scientists work in labs, wear white coats, conduct experiments, write up their results, and so on. Another service, called *Metaphor Eyes*, remedies this deficiency by employing a propositional model of the world that reasons with *subject-relation-object* triples rather than *subject-attribute* pairs. *Metaphor Eyes* acquires its world-model from a variety of sources (see Veale & Li, 2011), but the most fascinating of these sources is a niche Web-service offered (until recently) by the Google search-engine.

Many users of Web search-engines still enter full NL questions as search queries, even though most engines do not perform syntactic analysis. The Google engine maintains a record of frequently-posed queries and helpfully suggests apt completions for any familiar-seeming inputs. Google also provides a *completions service* (now sadly defunct) through which one may automatically retrieve the most common completions for any given query stub. The pairing of these observations – full NL questions plus the availability of common completions – allows a computer to acquire a propositional model of the world by polling Google for completions to question stubs of the form "*Why do Xs* ...". Why-do questions are remarkably revealing about the beliefs that we take for granted when speaking to others. The query "*Why do dogs bury bones*" tells us more than the fact that some dogs bury bones; it tells us that the questioner presupposes this to also be a fact held by the addressees of the query, and so it is a stereotypical generalization over all dogs. By repeating polling Google for completions of the query "Why do Xs", where X is any concept the system wishes to flesh out, *Metaphor Eyes* acquires a large body of common-sense beliefs.

Metaphor Eyes retrieves apt vehicles for a given a tenor concept **T** using the simple CIR query "**?T**". Thus, given *philosopher* as a tenor, *Metaphor Eyes* considers *scholar*, *moralist*, *theologian*, *historian*, *scientist*, *visionary*, *explorer*, *thinker*, *sage*, *pundit*, *poet* and even *warrior* as possible vehicles for a copula metaphor. For any given vehicle it then attempts to accommodate its knowledge of that vehicle into its representation of the tenor, by considering which propositions associated with the vehicle can be turned into apt propositions about the tenor. Consider the choice of *explorer* as a vehicle, producing the copula metaphor *philosophers are explorers*. Knowing that explorers perform wanderings, go on quests and seek knowledge, *Metaphor Eyes* looks for evidence in the Google n-grams that one or more of these propositions can just as well be said of philosophers. The 3-gram "philosopher's quest" attests to the aptness of the proposition "philosophers go on quests", while the 3-gram "philosopher's knowledge" attests to "philosophers look for knowledge". The 2-gram "wandering philosopher" additionally attests to the proposition that philosophers perform wanderings of their own.

Metaphor Eyes views metaphor as a representational lever, allowing it to fill the holes in its weak understanding of one concept by importing relevant knowledge from a neighboring concept. As such, in offering a partial solution to metaphor as a *problem*, it simultaneously views metaphor as a an acquisition *solution* in its own right. The *Metaphor Eyes* service can be accessed here:

http://boundinanutshell.com/metaphor-eye/

7 Stereotrope Poetry Generation

The copula form "X is a Y" is metaphor at its simplest and its purest, which perhaps explains why the form is far more prevalent in the metaphor literature than it is in real texts. Metaphor in the wild thrives in a wide variety of syntactic forms and rhetorical guises, with the most creatively rhetorical found in poetry. Yet while metaphors are the stuff of poetry, a well-written poem is much more than a bag of fancy metaphors. Coherent poems are driven by a coherent *master* metaphor, a schema that governs a poet's choice of related metaphors to elaborate this core idea.

A key benefit of the SOA philosophy is that services represent modular chunks of solution logic that need not, and do not, do everything for themselves. Ideally, our Web services should be reusable modules that can be composed, mashed-up and further elaborated by other developers to yield new services. In this spirit, *Stereotrope* is a service that generates poems from the metaphors produced by the *Metaphor Magnet* Web service.

Given a topic on which to wax poetically, *Stereotrope* calls on *Metaphor Magnet* to suggest a master metaphor around which its poem might be organized. Suppose our topic is *love*, and that *Metaphor Magnet* responds with, among others, the trope *Love is a Fire* (this copula metaphor has a frequency of 331 in the Google n-grams). Choosing this familiar trope as the core of its poem, *Stereotrope* now asks *Metaphor Magnet* to produce elaborations of this metaphor. *Metaphor Magnet* generates elaborations of *Love is a Fire* that include *Love is a Shining Flame*, *Love is a Dazzling Explosion* and *Love is a Raging Cauldron*. These elaborations – once rendered in the typical rhetorical forms of poetry – are then packaged by *Stereotrope* into a complete poem.

A useful rhetorical device is the *Superlative*. For instance, Metaphor Magnet suggests that for *Love is a Fire*, the properties *hot*, *bright* and *burning* can all be sensibly projected from *Fire* onto *Love* (as attested by the Google n-grams). The explicit statement *Love is a Fire* lacks a certain something in a poem, yet the same meaning can be suggested with the superlative forms "*No fire is hotter*" or "*No fire is brighter*". By looking to attested combinations in the Google n-grams, *Stereotrope* notices that "brightly" is an adverb that frequently modifies "burning", and so it also suggests the superlative "*No fire burns more brightly*". Yet by also noting that *hot* and *bright* are mutually reinforcing properties, since *bright* $\in$ *?hot*, it sees that the line "*No fire is hotter or burns more brightly*" will squeeze all three projected properties of *Fire* into a single superlative.

Stereotrope also calls upon the *Metaphor Eyes* Web-service to provide a proposition-level understanding of the world, for its poems must do more than allude to just the properties of entities. Unfortunately, banality is tacitly a pre-condition for the inclusion of almost any generalization in a common-sense knowledge-base. For it is precisely because so many of us tacitly share these beliefs that they are so worthy of inclusion in a knowledge-base and so unworthy of mention in a poem that rises above the obvious. Yet with the right rhetorical packaging, even a boring generalization can be pushed into the realm of the provocative, allowing an automated poetry system to temporarily slip the surly bonds of reality.

Consider the generalization "*celebrities ride in limousines*". Though it may fail to provoke when baldly expressed in this form, *Stereotrope* notes that *limousines* have some interesting qualities. They are typically *long*, for one, and though it does not believe celebrities to be typically short, it notes from the Google n-grams that the 2-gram "*short celebrities*" is also frequent enough to be an interesting talking point. Combining these two observations, it generates the rhetorical question "*Why do the shortest celebrities ride in the longest limousines?*". Though *Stereotrope* has no real insight into the frailty of celebrity egos, vertically challenged or otherwise, it is attracted to the elegant opposition of *long* vs. *short* that can be injected into this otherwise banal generalization.

As a rule, *Stereotrope* attempts to shoehorn a provocative opposition into any proposition that is said to be topic-relevant by *Metaphor Eyes*. Thus, knowing that arrows are fired from bows, that bows are *curved* and that arrows are *straight*, it generates the rhetorical question "*Why do the most curved bows fire the straightest arrows?*". The point is to suggest a more profound meaning beneath the surface. For when Don Corleone tells us that a fish rots from the head, he is not really talking about fish, but about how power corrupts an organization from the top down. Banal facts, when expressed in the right way, allude to a figurative meaning greater than themselves. By packaging its meagre facts in a rhetorical guise, *Stereotrope* can allude to a poetic meaning that lies outside its own power to comprehend.

Stereotrope generates the following poem from the master metaphor *Marriage is a Prison*:

The legalized regime of this marriage

My marriage is an emotional prison
Barred visitors do marriages allow
The most unitary collective scarcely organizes so much
Intimidate me with the official regulation of your prison
Let your sexual degradation charm me
Did ever an offender go to a more oppressive prison?
You confine me as securely as any locked prison cell
Does any prison punish more harshly than this marriage?
You punish me with your harsh security
The most isolated prisons inflict the most difficult hardships
Marriage, you disgust me with your undesirable security

Since the *Stereotrope* service complements the products of *Metaphor Magnet* (and *Metaphor Eyes*), it is engaged for each individual output of *Metaphor Magnet* directly. Thus, once again see:

http://boundinanutshell.com/metaphor-magnet-acl

8 The Flux Capacitor

The landmark television series *Breaking Bad* showcases story-telling at its most dramatic and its most transformational. It tells the tale of put-upon family man Walter White, a scientist with a brilliant mind who is trapped in the colorless life of a high-school chemistry teacher. When Walt is diagnosed with terminal lung cancer, he throws suburban caution to the wind and embraces a life of crime, first as a drug chemist of blue crystal meth and later as the ruthless drug baron *Heisenberg*. Walt's transformation, "from Mister Chips to Scarface" (in the words of the show's creator Vince Gilligan) is psychologically compelling because it is so unexpected yet so strongly rooted in our common-sense notions of similarity: for a drug chemist and a chemistry teacher share many of the same skills, while a drug baron embodies many of the same moral flaws as a drug chemist.

Literary transformations are often freighted with metaphorical meaning. Just think of the transformations of people into apt animals or plants in Ovid's *Metamorphoses*, or of Gregor Samsa's sudden, shame-driven transformation into a "gigantic vermin" in Franz Kafka's *Metamorphosis*. In *Breaking Bad*, where Walt's central transformation is slow-burning rather than magically immediate, a literal transformation is explained by the same kind of similarity judgments that motivate many of our metaphors. A service for producing apt metaphors, rooted in meaningful similarities, can thus be re-purposed to instead propose unexpected-but-apt character arcs for psychologically-compelling stories.

The *Flux Capacitor* is a new Web-service-in-development that re-packages the outputs of the *Metaphor Eyes* and *Metaphor Magnet* services as literal character transformations for use in computer-generated stories. The *Flux Capacitor* is thus conceived as a middleware service whose outputs are intended as inputs to other services. It does not package its outputs as metaphors, and nor does it package them as finished stories: rather, embracing the SOA philosophy of modularity and reuse, it produces Hollywood-style *pitches* that may underpin an interesting narrative that is to be fleshed out by another service or system.

Walter White's journey from chemistry teacher to drug baron is made believable by similarity, but it is made stimulating by *dissimilarity*. Like the best metaphors, a thought-provoking character transformation marries states that are both similar and incongruously dissimilar. The *Flux Capacitor* thus ranks the metaphors it receives from other services by their ability to surprise: a character arc from A to B is all the more surprising if our stereotype of A has properties that conflict with those in our stereotype of B. So the *Flux Capacitor* suggests the transformation of a scientist into a priest, or of a nun into a prostitute, or a king into a slave, or a fool into a philosopher, to capitalize on the dramatic possibilities of the oppositions that emerge in each case. The property-level interpretations of a character arc are given by *Metaphor Magnet*, while proposition-level insights are given by *Metaphor Eyes*.

The *Flux Capacitor* uses a variety of other techniques to ensure the meaningfulness of its proposed character arcs. For instance, it uses semantic knowledge to ensure that no transformation will change the gender of a character, and pragmatic knowledge to ensure that no transformation will reverse the age of a character. The *Flux Capacitor* is at present still being tested, but will soon be deployed as its own public Web service, where it may find useful work as a pitcher of new ideas to story-generation systems.

9 Out of the Mouths of Babes and Bots

The services described in this paper all operate in *pull* mode, where figurative products are generated on demand for the 3rd-party systems or users that ask for them. Each service produces HTML for human users and XML for automated queries.

We conclude this paper then by discussing an alternative model that has been overlooked here: a *push* mode of operation in which services broadcast their outputs, hopeful but unsolicited, to users or systems that may find some serendipitous value in being surprised in this way. Twitter is the ideal midwife for pushing automated metaphors into the world. For Twitter supports *twitterbots*, automated systems (or *bots*) that generate their own tweets, largely for the consumption and edification of human Twitter users. A new *twitterbot* named ***MetaphorIsMyBusiness*** (handle: ***@MetaphorMagnet***) employs all of the services described in previous sections to generate a novel creative metaphor every hour, on the hour.

@MetaphorMagnet's outputs are the product of a complex reasoning process that combines a comprehensive knowledge-base of stereotypical norms with real usage data from the Google n-grams. Though encouraged by the quality of its outputs, we continue to expand its expressive range, to give the twitterbot its own unique voice and identifiable aesthetic. Outputs such as "*What is an accountant but a timid visionary? What is a visionary but a bold accountant?*" lend the bot a sardonic persona that we wish to develop further.

We have seen the advantages to packaging metaphor systems as Web services, but there are also real advantages to packing metaphor Web-services as twitterbots. For one, the existence of mostly random bots that make no use of world knowledge or of metaphor theory – such as the playfully subversive *@metaphorminute* bot – provides a competitive baseline against which to evaluate the meaningfulness and value of the insights that are pushed out into the world by theory-driven / knowledge-driven twitterbots like *@MetaphorMagnet*. For another, the willingness of human Twitter users to *follow* such accounts regardless of their provenance, and to *retweet* the best outputs from these accounts, provides an empirical framework for estimating (and promoting) the figurative quality of the back-end Web services in each case. Finally, such bots may reap some social value in their own right, as sources of occasional insight, wit or profundity, or even of useful metaphors that are subsequently valued, adopted, and re-worked by human speakers.

References

Barnden, J. A. (2006). Artificial Intelligence, figurative language and cognitive linguistics. In: G. Kristiansen, M. Achard, R. Dirven, and F. J. Ruiz de Mendoza Ibanez (Eds.), *Cognitive Linguistics: Current Application and Future Perspectives*, 431-459. Berlin: Mouton de Gruyter.

Brants, T. and Franz, A. (2006). *Web 1T 5-gram Ver. 1*. Linguistic Data Consortium.

Erl, T. (2008). *SOA: Principles of Service Design.* Prentice Hall.

Fass, D. (1991). Met*: a method for discriminating metonymy and metaphor by computer. *Computational Linguistics*, 17(1):49-90.

Fass, D. (1997). Processing Metonymy and Metaphor. *Contemporary Studies in Cognitive Science & Technology*. New York: Ablex.

Fellbaum, C. (ed.) (1998). *WordNet: An Electronic Lexical Database*. MIT Press, Cambridge.

Fishelov, D. (1992). Poetic and Non-Poetic Simile: Structure, Semantics, Rhetoric. *Poetics Today*, 14(1), 1-23.

Hanks, P. (2006). Metaphoricity is gradable. In: Anatol Stefanowitsch and Stefan Th. Gries (Eds.), *Corpus-Based Approaches to Metaphor and Metonymy*,. 17-35. Berlin: Mouton de Gruyter.

Hearst, M. (1992). Automatic acquisition of hyponyms from large text corpora. *In Proc. of the 14th International Conference on Computational Linguistics*, pp 539–545.

Lakoff, G. and Johnson, M. (1980). *Metaphors We Live By*. University of Chicago Press.

Martin, J. H. (1990). A Computational Model of Metaphor Interpretation. New York: Academic Press.

Mason, Z. J. (2004). CorMet: A Computational, Corpus-Based Conventional Metaphor Extraction System, *Computational Linguistics*, 30(1):23-44.

Mihalcea, R. (2002). The Semantic Wildcard. In *Proc. of the LREC Workshop on Creating and Using Semantics for Information Retrieval and Filtering*. Canary Islands, Spain, May 2002.

Miller, G. A. and Charles, W. G. (1991). Contextual correlates of semantic similarity. *Language and Cognitive Processes* **6**(1):1-28.

Navigli, R. and Velardi, P. (2003). An Analysis of Ontology-based Query Expansion Strategies. In Proc. of the workshop on Adaptive Text Extraction and Mining (ATEM 2003), at ECML 2003, the 14th European Conf. on Machine Learning, 42–49.

Salton, G. (1968). *Automatic Information Organization and Retrieval*. New York: McGraw-Hill.

Shutova, E. (2010). Metaphor Identification Using Verb and Noun Clustering. In *the Proc. of the 23rd International Conference on Computational Linguistics*, 1001-1010.

Taylor, A. (1954). Proverbial Comparisons and Similes from California. *Folklore Studies* 3. Berkeley: University of California Press.

Taylor, M. R. (2009). *Marcel Duchamp: Étant donnés* (Philadelphia Museum of Art). Yale University Press.

Turney, P.D. and Littman, M.L. (2005). Corpus-based learning of analogies and semantic relations. *Machine Learning* 60(1-3):251-278.

Van Rijsbergen, C. J. (1979). *Information Retrieval.* Oxford: Butterworth-Heinemann.

Veale, T. (2004). The Challenge of Creative Information Retrieval. *Computational Linguistics and Intelligent Text Processing: Lecture Notes in Computer Science*, Volume 2945/2004, 457-467.

Veale, T. and Hao, Y. (2007a). Making Lexical Ontologies Functional and Context-Sensitive. *In Proc. of the 46th Annual Meeting of the Assoc. of Computational Linguistics.*

Veale, T. and Hao, Y. (2007b). Comprehending and Generating Apt Metaphors: A Web-driven, Case-based Approach to Figurative Language. *In Proc. of the 22nd AAAI Conf. on A.I.* Vancouver, Canada.

Veale, T. (2011). Creative Language Retrieval: A Robust Hybrid of Information Retrieval and Linguistic Creativity. Proceedings of ACL'2011, the 49th Annual Meeting of the Association of Computational Linguistics. June 2011.

Veale, T. and Li, G. (2011). Creative Introspection and Knowledge Acquisition: Learning about the world thru introspective questions and exploratory metaphors. In Proc. of the 25th AAAI Conf. of the Assoc. for Advancement of A.I., San Francisco.

Veale, T. and Li, G. (2013). Creating Similarity: Lateral Thinking for Vertical Similarity Judgments. *In Proceedings of ACL 2013, the 51st Annual Meeting of the Association for Computational Linguistics,* Sofia, Bulgaria, August 2013.

Veale, T. (2013). A Service-Oriented Architecture for Computational Creativity. *Journal of Computing Science and Engineering, 7(3):159-167.*

Voorhees, E. M. (1998). Using WordNet for text retrieval. *WordNet, An Electronic Lexical Database*, 285–303. The MIT Press.

Way, E. C. (1991). Knowledge Representation and Metaphor. *Studies in Cognitive systems*. Holland: Kluwer.

Wilks, Y. (1978). Making Preferences More Active, *Artificial Intelligence* 11.

Author Index